DEVELOPMENT CENTRE STUDIES

INVESTING
IN FREE EXPORT
PROCESSING ZONES

BY

ANTOINE BASILE ET DIMITRI GERMIDIS

DEVELOPMENT CENTRE
OF THE ORGANISATION FOR ECONOMIC CO-OPERATION AND DEVELOPMENT

Pursuant to article 1 of the Convention signed in Paris on 14th December, 1960, and which came into force on 30th September, 1961, the Organisation for Economic Co-operation and Development (OECD) shall promote policies designed:

- to achieve the highest sustainable economic growth and employment and a rising standard of living in Member countries, while maintaining financial stability, and thus to contribute to the development of the world economy;
- to contribute to sound economic expansion in Member as well as non-member countries in the process of economic development; and
- to contribute to the expansion of world trade on a multilateral, non-discriminatory basis in accordance with international obligations.

The Signatories of the Convention on the OECD are Austria, Belgium, Canada, Denmark, France, the Federal Republic of Germany, Greece, Iceland, Ireland, Italy, Luxembourg, the Netherlands, Norway, Portugal, Spain, Sweden, Switzerland, Turkey, the United Kingdom and the United States. The following countries acceded subsequently to this Convention (the dates are those on which the instruments of accession were deposited): Japan (28th April, 1964), Finland (28th January, 1969), Australia (7th June, 1971) and New Zealand (29th May, 1973).

The Socialist Federal Republic of Yugoslavia takes part in certain work of the OECD (agreement of 28th October, 1961).

The Development Centre of the Organisation for Economic Co-operation and Development was established by decision of the OECD Council on 23rd October, 1962.

The purpose of the Centre is to bring together the knowledge and experience available in Member countries of both economic development and the formulation and execution of general policies of economic aid; to adapt such knowledge and experience to the actual needs of countries or regions in the process of development and to put the results at the disposal of the countries by appropriate means.

The Centre has a special and autonomous position within the OECD which enables it to enjoy scientific independence in the execution of its task. Nevertheless, the Centre can draw upon the experience and knowledge available in the OECD in the development field.

Publié en français sous le titre :

**INVESTIR DANS LES ZONES FRANCHES
INDUSTRIELLES D'EXPORTATION**

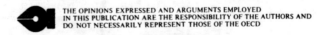

Edinburgh University
Library

This study is the final product of the research project "Policies to attract export oriented investment" as part of a broader research programme on "Foreign Investment and International Banking Activities in Developing Countries". It mainly synthesizes the work of a group of experts (listed on page 8) but takes account of other related material. Research was initiated in 1980 and involved the co-operation of researchers and Institutions in ten developing countries and two OECD Member countries.

Also available

NEW FORMS OF INTERNATIONAL INVESTMENT IN DEVELOPING COUNTRIES by Charles Oman
(41 84 02 1) ISBN 92-64-12590-6 140 pages   £6.50   US$13.00   F65.00

WORLD ECONOMIC INTERDEPENDENCE AND THE EVOLVING NORTH-SOUTH RELATIONSHIP (May 1983)
(43 83 04 1) ISBN 92-64-12446-2 84 pages   £4.50   US$9.00   F45.00

INTERNATIONAL SUBCONTRACTING: A NEW FORM OF INVESTMENT (January 1981)
(41 80 08 1) ISBN 92-64-12129-3 228 pages   £5.40   US$13.50   F54.00

Prices charged at the OECD Publications Office.

THE OECD CATALOGUE OF PUBLICATIONS and supplements will be sent free of charge on request addressed either to OECD Publications Office, 2, rue André-Pascal, 75775 PARIS CEDEX 16, or to the OECD Sales Agent in your country.

TABLE OF CONTENTS

Part one

DIRECT FOREIGN INVESTMENT AND DEVELOPMENT POLICIES

I. DIRECT FOREIGN INVESTMENT AND THE INDUSTRIALISATION PROCESS

II. EXPORT OBJECTIVES AND FREE EXPORT PROCESSING ZONES (FEPZ)

Part two

INTERFACE BETWEEN ENTERPRISE STRATEGIES AND HOST COUNTRY STRATEGIES

III. ENTREPRISE STRATEGIES

IV. HOST COUNTRY STRATEGIES

V. INCENTIVES AND CONSTRAINTS

Part three

RECONCILATION OF OBJECTIVES AND "BALANCED ARRANGEMENTS"

VI. STATIC APPROACH - BRAKING EFFECTS AND STIMULATING EFFECTS

VII.   DYNAMICS OF SPECIALISATION AND ACQUIRED ADVANTAGES

LIST OF TABLES

Tables

ACKNOWLEDGMENTS

The authors express their thanks to :

— Messrs. Emmanuel Jahan, Claudio Jedlicki, Mario Lanzarotti, Jean Masini (France)
— Mrs. Mona Ghaled Mourad and Mr. Farouk Shakweer (Egypt)
— Mr. Fernando Gonzales Vigil (Peru)
— Mr. Chan-Jin Kim (Korea)
— Mr. Mark Lester (Philippines and Malaysia)
— Mr. Patrick Nugawela (Sri Lanka)
— Mr. Eustaquio J. Reis (Brazil)
— Mr. Prakash Tandon (India)
— Mr. Guillermo Teutli Otero (Mexico)

who have contributed decisively to the realisation of this study, both by participating actively in the work of the group of experts, and by providing the Development Centre with useful primary data for each of the countries shown in brackets.

Their thanks are extended also to the Culture Learning Institute of the East-West Center of Hawaii, to USAID (Egypt) and to the Institut de l'Entreprise (France) and IEDES at the Paris-I University and to all the research institutions in developing countries which have collaborated in the execution of the research.

8

PREFACE

The selection of effective strategies for industrialisation is a matter of some complexity. In the 1960s and 1970s, it was thought that industrialisation might be set in train most easily by replacing imported manufactured goods with domestic production protected from foreign competition by tariffs and other means. Experience showed that this could have the serious drawback of resulting in unsound and non-competitive industrial structures. By contrast it was found possible, for example in the Korean experience, that export-orientated industries of foreign origin could be established and succeed in becoming competitive and capturing world markets. This has given new emphasis to the search for means to attract foreign industry. The establishment of Free Export Processing Zones is intended to do this by attracting international industry to areas in which goods may be imported freely without the payment of customs duties and processed for export markets with a minimum of restrictions.

A variety of interests in the activities of such Zones may be discerned. On the one hand, the host governments see them as a valuable means to create employment, transfer technology and improve the balance of payments. The governments of the countries from which the companies originate, on the other hand, may be concerned by an apparent loss of employment opportunities and acquired technological advantages. Moreover, while companies in the Free Export Processing Zone expect to secure advantages from establishing themselves there, local firms may be affected — unfavourably or favourably — in a variety of ways. This study is thus set in an international context where conflicting interests amongst the parties concerned have to be reconciled. By throwing light on the complex problems of industrial economic interdependence between developing and developed countries, the study may also be seen as a contribution to the North-South dialogue.

Important issues are at stake. Free Export Processing Zones are proliferating throughout the world ; the competition to attract industry to them (as expressed in the adoption of extremely liberal foreign investment regimes), has resulted in under-utilisation of the infrastructure created to receive it, leading to the waste of already scarce resources. Such considerations make it urgently necessary to examine the situation with a view to adopting remedial measures. As the authors rightly emphasize in their conclusions, such measures must be integrated into a conscious and enlightened economic policy that is set in a dynamic perspective in which the need for changing patterns of industrial specialisation is accepted.

The study was conducted in association with many research institutions and financial agencies in the countries covered by this research : Korea, Philippines, Malaysia, Sri Lanka, India, Lebanon, Egypt, Mexico, Peru, Brazil, France and the United States. Its operational relevance is already evident. In India, following the work of our consultant (the author of the Indian case study), a committee on "free zones and 100 per cent export units" was set up in the Ministry of Commerce under the chairmanship of our consultant

9

to review the framework for creating such zones. In Peru, our study was used for the debate that took place on the creation of free zones as part of the Government's liberal policy. In Egypt, our consultant was appointed adviser to the Minister of Economy with special responsibility for questions of free zones.

I trust that this work will constitute a useful instrument for policy-makers as well as business circles, both in developing and developed countries, thus contributing to the economic development of developing countries.

Just Faaland
President, OECD Development Centre.
April, 1984

INTRODUCTION

The increasing interest taken by many developing countries in policies to attract export-oriented investment is prompted by a dual concern. The aim is on the one hand to attract foreign investment, which is expected to provide foreign outlets, create jobs, transfer technology and know-how, generate inflow of foreign exchange, etc. and on the other hand, to promote a whole process of specifically national industrialisation in a protected domestic market. This dual attitude has led to the preparation and adoption of direct foreign investment systems of a dualist nature. It contains an inherent basic contradiction, insofar as the host country, in dissociating the domestic market from the export market, is not certain to obtain from the foreign investment the advantages which it could legitimately expect.

Consequently the problem is to make a correct and precise analysis of the goals pursued by the host country. This approach is essential if the institutional, physical and administrative instruments and infrastructure are to be designed, executed and adapted accordingly.

The dual constraint, which is analysed in terms of objectives and strategies specific to the host country on the one hand and to the investor enterprise on the other, is particularly well illustrated in the institution of the "Free Export Processing Zone" (referred to hereafter as FEPZ).

The interest of this institution from the standpoint of the approach adopted is not limited to its contribution in purely analytical terms, but is linked to the increasingly frequent use made of it by many developing countries which regard it as the most promising instrument of their industrialisation and greater integration into international trade. The considerable and relatively recent proliferation of FEPZ throughout the world is ample proof of this, and much may be learnt from their experience.

Apart from a cost-benefit evaluation in static terms we shall seek to determine as precisely as possible the objective conditions to be achieved by the host country. These should make the FEPZ and more generally any policy to attract export-oriented foreign investment, the preferred instrument for changing the economic structures of the country concerned in line with the reasoned objectives of its industrialisation and development.

It will then be possible to try to reconcile the strategies pursued by the host country on the one hand and the investor enterprise on the other hand, these strategies having been previously identified and analysed. Reconciliation will be based on well understood interests, which are the best guarantee of real lasting co-operation adapted to the many and changing requirements of the host country. These requirements correspond to the acquisition of ever higher comparative advantages in the hierarchy of international specialisation, an achievement which will have been made possible by external contributions made through the investor enterprise.

The group of experts has made a substantial contribution to this study. Nevertheless, considerable difficulties were encountered, some theoretical or methodological, others practical. On the one hand, there are very few antecedents in theoretical or methodological analyses to date ; on the other hand data, where available, are very heterogeneous.

There are two further difficulties in data collection. The first concerns the different ages of zones ; some are at the beginning of their life cycle, others are moving towards the end. In such conditions it seems difficult to draw up general "balance sheets". The second relates to the nature of the free zone. For countries which have opted for FEPZ "status" without the "geographical enclave" character, statistics relating to enterprises operating under this status are not always separate from data on foreign enterprises in general.

Since some of the studies cover certain specific aspects of free zones (for example, those on the Philippines and Malaysia deal above all with the technology transfer problem), it has not been possible for us to obtain statistical series concerning the magnitude of certain factors (for example, technology, skills, value added, etc.) for the whole group of countries.

Lastly, the existence in various papers of a global assessment unaccompanied by detailed statistics on certain aspects of free zones, while allowing us to derive some general conclusions, has at times prevented us from consolidating them statistically.

Our approach comprised three stages which form the three parts of the study :

Part one : Direct foreign investment and development policy. Part two : Interface between enterprise strategies and host country strategies. Part three : Reconciliation of objectives and "balanced" arrangements.

Part one

DIRECT FOREIGN INVESTMENT AND DEVELOPMENT POLICIES

The attention of the economic development expert has tended to shift from the analysis of international flows of goods and services to the monitoring of capital movements and the process of direct foreign investment. This trend has occurred as a result of the changes in the state of international economic relationships revealing the greater relative importance of direct foreign investment in the restructuring of international trade.

The developing countries receiving direct investment from the most advanced economies saw an opportunity enabling them to achieve their industrialisation objectives by providing them with the production factors they lacked. However their attitude to the foreign investor did not remain neutral being mainly conditioned by the concern to maximise the positive effects of the investment while minimising the constraints it imposed on the national economy. In addition the industrialisation strategies adopted were modified, with an export-oriented strategy prevailing over import substitution ; this has prompted change in the policies of the foreign investor.

The changes described led the host countries to devise instruments of co-operation with the foreign enterprise, endeavouring to reconcile the requirements of their own development with the enterprise's concerns. This was the context in which there emerged the institution of "Free Export Processing Zone" which is at the centre of our analysis.

I. DIRECT FOREIGN INVESTMENT
AND THE INDUSTRIALISATION PROCESS

Direct foreign investment is considered by most developing host countries as a major instrument of their industrialisation. This prompted various attitudes reflecting both choices inherent in the economic system adopted and choices relating to desired objectives and economic policies.

However promotion of exports of manufactured goods prevailed over all other economic policy considerations, leading to a considerable development of free export processing zone.

A. Diversity of host country attitudes

Several types of attitude to foreign investment can be distinguished, corresponding to different choices of objectives in economic policy, foreign investment control and investment promotion.

13

1. Objectives and means

A definition of the probable attitudes is only possible through a detailed analysis of the different components of the host country policy with regard to foreign investment. These components relate not only to the socio-economic and purely economic aims, but also to the means of implementing the policy in question.

Socio-economic objectives include the following :

- National control of mechanisms for allocating natural and human resources, acquired or not.
- Less foreign dependence for certain inputs, such as expertise, technology, research and development and certain goods and services.
- Diversification of foreign factors of production.
- More balanced distribution of income, geographically or among the various population categories.
- Achievement of a satisfactory population balance, by provoking or preventing internal and/or external migration.
- Promotion of greater participation of the workforce in enterprise capital and/or decision-making.
- General improvement of the level of employment, quantitatively and qualitatively.
- Achievement of greater integration in international and/or regional trade flows.

A non-exhaustive list of economic objectives may include :

- Use of "appropriate technology" ;
- Economies of scale at the level of production units ;
- Improvement of competition in the country concerned ;
- Recourse to relatively less onerous foreign inputs : financial resources, technology, expertise, other resources ;
- Achievement of better balance-of-payments equilibrium, notably by increasing exports ;
- Improvement of local capabilities, notably by training on the job or under pre-established programmes.

The means developed to achieve the above objectives have a direct impact on foreign investment policy. They include both direct control of foreign investment by the host country and sets of constraints and incentives likely to condition and guide foreign investment.

In the first case, control may be exercised in two ways, either through participation in decisions regarding foreign investment e.g. profit reinvestment, or secondly through intervention by the host country authorities in contracts concerning industrial co-operation, turnkey operations, acquisition of patents, trademarks, reproduction, know-how.

In the second case — constraints and incentives affecting foreign investment — we may mention measures concerning exchange control, investment restrictions (by sector, function, region or size of enterprise), various guarantees (regarding nationalisation or expropriation, breach of contract, international arbitration, discrimination) financial and fiscal incentives, subsidies, domestic market protection...

2. Different types of attitudes

The many combinations of the various components described enable us to identify the possible attitudes of the host country to foreign investment. The categories retained should however be interpreted with caution. On the one hand, they are in no case completely clearcut in reality. On the other hand, there are certainly attitudes presenting some analogies with the different categories retained. A possible typology is set out below in order of increasing restriction.

First type of attitude

This corresponds to the widest possible opening to foreign investment, but does not mean that it is not controlled at all. Even the most liberal countries reserve investment in certain sectors for their nationals, or at least require that foreign participation in the enterprise's capital should not exceed a certain level. The most strictly controlled sectors in this respect are generally the defence industries, energy, mining and quarrying, transport and telecommunications, real estate — i.e. what might be regarded as strategic sectors.

Although few countries in this first category limit the acquisition of foreign technology and know-how through contracts, most of them impose restrictions on the employment of foreign personnel. Moreover, many of them protect certain domestic activities through tariff and non-tariff barriers or simply by prohibition. Lastly, they often impose a licensing system for the export of certain products or technologies on grounds of internal considerations such as national defence or political relations with the country of destination.

The incentives offered to the foreign investor are often limited to the less developed regions and are generally modest. The case of Lebanon is a good illustration of this first type of attitude to foreign investment.

Second type of attitude

Countries in this category are less liberal than those in the first category insofar as they require the direct foreign investment to be declared and registered. Often, as in the case of Venezuela, they require the investment to be accompanied by technology transfer contracts.

Investment incentives not related to a certain location are designed to guide investment and the relevant technology in a direction likely to serve the national objectives. These incentives may take various forms such as subsidies or tax facilities, or both. The number of sectors open to direct foreign investment varies according to the case.

In general this second category focusses more on incentives for direct foreign investment than on restrictions.

Third type of attitude

Unlike the countries in the previous categories, those in the third category undertake an evaluation of the foreign investment and its relevant technology before its acceptance. Although incentives are offered for desired investments, the emphasis is generally on restriction.

Foreign investment evaluation criteria and their importance vary considerably from country to country. Egypt for instance considers the impact on exchange reserves ; Mexico, value added and transfer of skills. Malaysia looks for the eventual association of local capital ; Nigeria considers the investment's conformity with national plans and its total amount ; South Korea is more concerned about non-competition with local enterprises.

These countries in general show a distinct preference for joint ventures. As regards technology imports, some of them, like Mexico, are very restrictive and tightly control payments of royalties and fees. The incentives offered are usually linked to performance levels with regard to export, employment, location, participation rate and value added.

Fourth type of attitude

Here, direct foreign investment is only possible under an agreement specifying the exact conditions which the investor must fulfil. In some cases, e.g. the Philippines and Sri Lanka, qualitative criteria are used to define the rules which the foreign investor must obey. These criteria are concerned more particularly with the required rate of local participation, management control, or the repatriation of profits, dividends, royalties and fees, and vary according to the sector and the degree of priority of the proposed investment.

Often a time limit will be set beyond which the foreign investor must cede his enterprise. This is the case in Indonesia and Peru. Often incentives will be maintained or suspended according to the positive or negative results obtained. If the cost/benefit ratio is low — i.e. favourable — more liberal provisions may be applied in various fields of interest to the investor — for example, in the Philippines, provisions relating to participation rate and management control ; or in Indonesia, provisions concerning recourse to international arbitration.

Fifth type of attitude

In these countries direct foreign investment is authorised only in the form of a contractual joint venture established in order to achieve a very specific objective in a given period of time. This is generally the attitude of the centrally planned economies of Eastern Europe, which nevertheless maintain a significant opening to the outside world. The foreign investor usually has only a minority participation in the capital of the venture, but is sometimes granted a right of veto in certain crucial areas.

Yugoslavia was the pioneer in this field and was followed by Hungary, Poland and Romania. Later in 1978 the People's Republic of China indicated its desire to admit foreign capital on roughly similar conditions.

The main difference between these various countries is in the degree of autonomy which national enterprises have in negotiating with foreign interests. Yugoslav enterprises seem to have the greatest effective autonomy. The People's Republic of China seems to be particularly attracted by the Yugoslav model.

In any case the foreign investment must fit in exactly with the objectives of the national plans and be fully compatible with existing laws. Whatever discretion partners may have at the time of negotiation, the final agreement remains subject to government approval.

Other attitudes

Two other categories of planned economy countries with different attitudes to foreign investment may also be described here. In the first case, as in the Soviet Union, only technology transfer contracts are authorised, and on certain conditions, to the exclusion of traditional forms of direct foreign investment. In the other case, as in Albania, both technology transfer contracts and direct foreign investment are categorically prohibited. These categories cannot of course concern our study.

B. Industrial policy issues

1. Industrialisation strategies

For a long time there were two contrasting industrialisation strategies and preference was given to one or other according to the prevailing economic circumstances. Industrialisation was either geared to import substitution or based on export promotion. In fact neither model was put into application without allowing some exceptions and nowhere was it possible to observe a model in the pure state. In general pragmatism prevailed and while the theorists' approach to the problems sounded dogmatic, the measures taken were essentially empirical.

a) The industrialisation process geared to import substitution

Up to the crisis of 1929 any process of economic development seemed to postulate the export of manufactured goods. The "great depression" marked a breaking-point, with most developing countries experiencing a sudden drop in their exports, substantial outflows of capital, and a sharp deterioration in their terms of trade with the outside world.

The Second World War made it difficult to supply the countries concerned with manufactured goods, both because of uncertainties of transfer and because of the collapse of production among their traditional suppliers. In addition these countries found their indebtedness increasing and their import-financing capacity decreasing due to the fall in international demand for many of the primary products that they exported.

Consequently the developing countries turned quite naturally to what was considered a more realistic policy of import substitution and this policy was systematically applied as from 1950. This trend was also accompanied by an increasing determination on the part of the countries concerned to free themselves from too great dependence on the outside world, and a policy of diversification through an industrialisation effort supported by infant industry protection seemed to be the best alternative.

This first re-orientation of industrial policy was very soon questioned due to the setbacks encountered. The main reason was that while it had been possible to reduce imports of manufactured goods, in particular consumer goods, the effect was more than offset by the increase in imports of intermediate products and capital goods essential to the industrialisation process. This led to considerable pressure on the balance of payments of the countries concerned.

Moreover, any attempt to export was henceforward compromised by high production costs due to customs barriers, a cost-raising factor ; and most enterprises, looking at the smallness of the domestic market, used only a minute fraction of their production capacity or set up sub-optimal production units[2]. The phenomenon was particularly noticeable in Latin America.

b) The export-based industrialisation process

With some qualifications, in general the failure of any industrial policy based on import substitution is manifest. Consequently we should not be surprised that even in 1975 51 out of 144 developing countries had turned resolutely to an export-oriented industrial policy[3]. And very soon for most of the Third World countries foreign trade became the mainspring of any industrial strategy.

This new industrial policy orientation of the developing countries was based on the availability of a plentiful supply of cheap labour. The countries which had the greatest success in this new path were those which could recruit plenty of disciplined workers, drawn from an agricultural sector which had prospered through rationalising and modernising farming techniques. The experience of Taiwan, Mexico, Korea and Brazil may be mentioned here, although different procedures were used.

The new industrialisation policy orientation followed by the developing countries in no way implied less State interference than in the import substitution process. State action simply followed other channels. Intervention was henceforward mainly at the level of infrastructures, incentives to enterprises playing a leading role in the industrialisation process, differentiated or selective openings for foreign investment, redefinition of customs and trade policy objectives, sound management of the labour force etc.

2. The concerns of industrialised countries

The two main vectors of industrial policy are still customs policy which must henceforward include franchises for inputs, including production components, and secondly a policy to attract foreign investment, which also implies favourable physical, administrative and social infrastructures.

a) Tariff provisions

In fact the opportunities offered for foreign enterprises to invest in developing countries are largely dependent on the tariff provisions in force in the investor's country of origin, more specifically when the proposed activity consists of assembly operations with a view to re-export to the country of origin.

Many industrialised countries have adopted the principle that components originating in the investor's country are not subject to any duty on their re-importation, so that duty is payable only on the work done abroad. Items 806.30 and 807.00 of the Tariff Schedules of the United States are relevant here[4].

The second Item, which is of more general scope than the first[5], provides that on condition that the products "have not lost their physical identity" abroad, processing may be carried out by non-US enterprises, that further processing in the United States is not necessary, and lastly, that foreign components can be combined with US components. Thus, the participation of local enterprises in the manufacturing process and the use of domestic components are encouraged. Among the developing countries particularly favoured in this respect are Mexico, Taïwan, Singapore, Malaysia and Hong Kong.

The Federal Republic of Germany has also provided tariff concessions for imports from non-EEC countries. In fact the countries that have benefited most in respect of assembly operations are the East European countries.

France too admits a certain number of products under the heading of "trafic de perfectionnement passif". These are chiefly articles of ready-made clothing from North Africa and especially Eastern Europe. Many other industrialised countries offer similar customs concessions which are supposed to benefit products from the developing countries.

There are also regional or international agreements favouring imports from the least developed countries — for instance, the Lomé Convention linking the EEC Member States with nearly 50 countries, mostly African, and the "Generalised System of Preferences" adopted by 19 OECD Member countries.

b)   The emergence of the Newly industrialising countries

After the recession of 1974-75 which affected all the advanced industrial countries and notably the OECD Member countries, the changes due to the emergence of the NICs became a matter of serious concern to advanced countries struggling against the combined effects of slow growth, high unemployment and balance of payments difficulties. At the same time the process of industrial adjustment was inadequate or rejected by the most advanced countries, the danger of a revival of protectionism drew nearer.

Such a development implies that instead of moving on from industrial activities for which the developing countries have an increasing competitive advantage to activities where their own competitiveness is greater, the advanced economies try to perpetuate the existing structure. By poor resource allocation they thus reduce the growth prospects of healthy industries.

The availability of potential investment capital resulting from the foreign exchange surpluses of the OPEC countries and the weakness of private demand for credit in the OECD countries certainly contributed decisively to the flow of investment to the developing countries, notably to those offering acceptable guarantees of solvency and showing some real dynamism.

The role of foreign capital differed considerably from one country to another and from one period to another. Nevertheless such flows obviously promoted the industrialisation of the NICs[6] adopting resolutely outward-looking growth strategies and policies. Thus OECD Member countries' imports from the NICs rose from US$ 1.2 billion in 1963 to 55 billion in 1979 and their import share from 2.6 per cent to 8.9 per cent[7].

II. EXPORT OBJECTIVES AND FREE EXPORT PROCESSING ZONES (FEPZ)

Foreign investment regimes, both in developed and developing countries, tend to have a dual character, regardless of whether specific investment codes have been adopted. This duality is due to the increasingly frequent differentiation of investments according to whether their product is intended exclusively for foreign markets or, conversely, mainly for the domestic market of the host country.

This division is all the more marked since a revival of economic protectionism is to be found all over the world. And we are then faced with a situation in which, in addition to investments obeying strict rules, there are more and more investments subject to a more liberal regime which are difficult to subject to a precise evaluation. Such investment tends to represent ever larger sectors of the national economies and the world economy.

The institution which reflects this phenomenon best is the "Free Export Processing Zone" (FEPZ).

FEPZ marks the convergence of two significant trends in the international division of labour.

The first relates to the will of certain countries to opt deliberately for an export-oriented development policy following the relative failure of a number of import substitution experiments. In this connection the creation of FEPZs is usually the preferred back-up for such a policy. This applies in particular to most of the Asian countries. In other cases however the introduction of FEPZs is grafted on to a less firmly outward looking policy, e.g. India and Mexico.

The second trend concerns the production cost minimisation strategy followed by enterprises in the industrialised countries which either seek to meet certain structural difficulties and remove increasing competitive pressures or try to maintain or even increase their competitiveness. These enterprises are then constrained to relocate part of their production capacity with a view to re-exporting their output either to their country of origin or abroad.

A. Definition and role of the FEPZ

1. Convergent concepts

A possible definition of the FEPZ is as follows :

"An administratively and sometimes geographically defined area, enjoying special status allowing for the free import of equipment and other materials to be used in the manufacture of goods earmarked for export. The special status generally involves favourable legal provisions and regulations pertaining mainly to taxation. Both the above constitute incentives for foreign investment."[8]

The more detailed definition given by the World Bank distinguishes the Export Processing Zone from the Free Trade Zone and is as follows :

"The export processing zone (EPZ) is a relatively recent variant of the widely used free trade zone (FTZ) — a designated area, usually in or next to a port area, to and from which unrestricted trade is permitted with the rest of the world. Merchandise may be moved in and out of FTZs free of customs, stored in warehouses for varying periods and repackaged as needed. Goods imported from the FTZ into the host country pay the requisite duty ; their prior storage in FTZ warehouses permits rapid delivery to order, meanwhile saving interest on customs payments.
FEPZs, more specifically, also provide buildings and services for manufacturing, i.e., transformation of imported raw and intermediate materials into finished products, usually for export but sometimes partly for domestic sale subject to the normal duty. The EPZ is thus a specialized industrial estate located physically and/or administratively outside the customs barrier, oriented to export production. Its facilities serve as a showcase to attract investors and a convenience for their getting established, and are usually associated with other incentives."[9]

In any case the FEPZ has two main characteristics :

— It is an "enclave" enjoying a status that does not extend to the whole territory of the country.
— Enterprises established there must export their production.

This would exclude from our definition the free ports[10] of Hong Kong and Singapore, which do not fulfil the first condition, as well as the free zones set up in the United States which do not fulfil the second.

2. A flexible instrument of industrial policy

The FEPZ tends to be regarded by developing countries as a necessary stage in their growth by stimulating exports of manufactured goods and/or specific services from specially created free zones which have the particular merit of attracting the capital which the country lacks. Into this melting-pot would flow foreign capital, know-how, technology, assured markets... This is very different from the time when the development process was essentially based on import-substitution industrialisation, a strategy recognised in most cases as inadequate.

It has in fact been established that, unless the internal market is very large, customs protection is bound to lead to very limited industrial development. Moreover, an industrial sector which has had the benefit of protective measures at the outset will have great difficulty in turning to the export market, since it has acquired no technical know-how nor the necessary marketing and management skills. In any case the creation of an FEPZ does not exclude an industrial policy based on import substitution. Some correlation can even be established between the importance of existing tariff protection and the development of exceptional systems including FEPZs. This is of course quite natural, as in a completely liberal system the FEPZ has no raison d'être.

B. Proliferation and problems of the FEPZ

1. Development of the FEPZ

There has been a remarkable proliferation of FEPZs in developing countries since 1966, when there were only two : Kandla in India and Mayaguez in Puerto Rico. In 1970 their number had risen to eight situated in eight countries : in addition to the previous two, Kaohsiung in Taiwan, Bataan in the Philippines, La Romana in the Dominican Republic, the zones along the Mexican border, Colon in Panama (now mainly a free trade zone) and Manaus in Brazil.

From 1971 to 1975[11] 23 zones were set up in 11 countries, mainly situated in Asia (nine in Malaysia, two in Taiwan, two in South Korea and one in India). In Central and South America three zones were established in Colombia, one in El Salvador and one in Guatemala. Over the same period three zones were set up in the Caribbean — two in the Dominican republic and one in Haiti ; and the first African zone was set up in Mauritius.

From 1976 to 1978[12] 21 zones were created, but the focus was now outside Asia where only Malaysia and Sri Lanka set up new zones, followed later by Thailand. On the other hand ten zones were set up in the Middle East (four in Egypt, five in Syria and one in Jordan).

Three African countries followed the example of Mauritius — Liberia, Senegal and Togo. Jamaica did the same, and in Central and South America, Belize, Honduras, Nicaragua and Chile. The Island of Samoa in the Pacific also set up a zone. Lastly, since 1979 China has been trying to develop free zones in the province of Canton (Shanzhen, Zhuhai and Shanteu).

In 1980[13] many projects were in the planning or developing stage — twenty one in Asia and Pacific, four in the Middle East and Europe, seven in Africa and three in the Carribean, Central and Latin America. Table 1, although not confined to FEPZs (it contains any free export zone in general), nevertheless gives an idea of their extensive development.

The developments described above may be attributed mainly to the following considerations :

- Location of industrial enterprises in the industrialised countries is becoming less and less profitable, both because of high wage costs and because of environmental protection measures.
- Development of production techniques enabling complex production processes to be broken down into components means that these can be entrusted to workers who are relatively unskilled or need only a little rapid training.
- Development of transport techniques (air freight, containers), tele-communications, computerised information technology etc, makes industrial location and production control less and less dependent on geographical distance.

Table 1. FREE EXPORT PROCESSING ZONES IN OPERATION
IN DEVELOPING COUNTRIES IN 1970 AND 1981

Country	1970	1981
Bahamas	1	1
Bangladesh		1
Barbados		1
Belize		1
Bermuda	1	1
Brazil	1	1
Chile		3
China		3
Colombia	1	3
Dominican republic	1	3
Egypt		4
El Salvador		1
Guatemala		1
Haiti		1
Honduras		1
India	1	2
Indonesia		2
Jamaica		1
South Korea		9[1]
Liberia		1
Malaysia	2	8
Malta		1
Mauritius	1	1
Mexico		25[2]
Nicaragua		1
Pakistan		1
Philippines		1
Senegal		1
Sri Lanka		1
Syria		4
Syria-Jordan		1
Taiwan	2	3
Tunisia		3
Venezuela		1
Total	11	96

1. Of which 7 export-oriented industrial estates.
2. Public and private.
   Sources : Diamond and Diamond, UNIDO 1980, Currie and others.

2. Unequal results

While certain FEPZs can be regarded as successful — more particularly Shannon (Ireland), Kaoshiung (Taiwan), Sungei Way and Bayan Lepas (Malaysia), Mauritius, Bataan (Philippines) Masan (South Korea) — there have been many notable failures. Considerable capacity remains unused in most zones, leading to the wastage of already scarce resources in the host countries concerned.

It may thus be feared that the spread of FEPZ may lead to a surge of competition among the countries concerned, each vying with the other in offering the most liberal status and excessive inducements with regard to tax concessions, exchange control, terms of credit and laxity in the regulation and control of the planned activities, either in the area of labour legislation, restrictive practices, or modes of appropriation. This could concern not only labour legislation and restrictive practices, but also appropriation methods. In the long run not only may the cost of inducements prove greater than the total benefits derived from the creation of the zone, but there may be a danger of the enterprises losing interest in the least privileged zones. Substantial investment, such as port installations, would thus be under-utilised.

Such developments are not necessarily of advantage to the enterprises established in the zones concerned, for in the end the quality of services, efficiency of equipment, and the necessary modernisation programmes, to be paid for by the zone authorities, might well be compromised.

It may be of interest here to mention that international agencies like UNCTAD and UNIDO, after warmly encouraging developing countries to set up FEPZs on their territory, subsequently became much more reserved and even extremely cautious in several cases. Between 1971 and 1973 these agencies regarded FEPZs and international subcontracting as a means of increasing and diversifying exports of manufactured goods from non-industrial countries. Subsequently they realised the possible consequences of excessive inter-zone competition due to the considerable increase in the number of FEPZs.

In 1970 UNIDO began to provide technical assistance for identifying and selecting individual export-oriented projects ; later it extended its assistance to the preparation of economic and technical feasibility studies for the creation of FEPZs in developing countries and advice on their implementation and management. Organising an investment promotion system in the zone, setting up the infrastructures, training zone administrators and evaluating industrial projects are also some of the tasks that UNIDO may undertake.

Working in co-operation with UNDP and UNCTAD, UNIDO has closely associated other bodies with its action, such as the Asian Productivity Organisation with its headquarters in Tokyo and the United States Flagstaff Institute. Moreover, a World Export Processing Zones Association was founded in 1978 with the aim of promoting and strengthening cooperation between EPZ authorities.

NOTES

1. See : Richard D. Robinson, "Foreign Investment in the Third World : A Comparative Study of Selected Development Country Investment Promotion Programs". International Division Chamber of Commerce of the U.S. 1980.

2. See Antoine E. Basile : "Commerce extérieur et Développement de la petite nation - Essai sur les contraintes de l'exiguité économique". Droz, Geneva, 1972.

3. See P. Judet : "Les nouveaux pays industriels", collection Nord-Sud. Édition Économie et Humanisme, 1981, p. 30.

4. See Sanjaya Iall : "Offshore assembly in developing countries" in National Westminter Bank Quarterly Review, London, reproduced in Problèmes Economiques N° 1713, 24th December 1980.

5. Item 806.30 concerns only metal manufactures.

6. Reference may be made to the countries selected by OECD, i.e. Brazil, Greece, Hong Kong, South Korea, Mexico, Portugal, Singapore, Spain and Taiwan, without thereby excluding other countries.

7. See. OECD : "The Impact of the Newly Industrialising Countries on Production and Trade in Manufactures", Updating of selected tables in the 1979 Report, Paris 1981.

8. The proposed definition is based mainly on UNIDO and UNCTAD studies.

9. See Carl Goderez : A World Bank Staff Working Paper on Export Processing Zones, pp. 7-8, 1981.

10. The World Export Processing Zones Association adopts a very wide definition : "all government authorized areas such as free ports, free trade zones, custom free zones, industrial free zones or foreign trade or any other type of zone, as the Council may from time to time decide to include." (Statutes of the World Export Processing Zones Association, ID/W.6/266/6, 28th February 1978).

11.   Currie J. "Investment : the growing role of export processing zones", the Economist Intelligence Unit, Special Report n° 64, London 1979.

12.   *Idem.*

13.   USAID "Free Zones in developing countries : expanding opportunities for the private sector" : Discussion Paper n° 18. Washington, November 1983.

Part two

INTERFACE BETWEEN ENTERPRISE STRATEGIES AND HOST COUNTRY STRATEGIES

The first prerequisite for the success of an FEPZ is its propensity to attract the foreign investor to set up in the zone, which will clearly depend largely on the extent to which the advantages offered by the zone in question meet the requirements of the investing enterprise. The various aspects of the latter's strategy will therefore have to be ascertained beforehand, otherwise the efforts made by the FEPZ — which can be analysed in terms of costs — will have been to no avail or entailed the waste of resources — already scarce in developing countries — and the loss of opportunities that will not arise again.

Thus, before calculating the probability of an FEPZ's success or failure, it would seem essential to compare the respective objectives and strategies of the investing enterprise and the host country.

III. ENTERPRISE STRATEGIES

As a first step the specific character of the investing enterprise should be determined, that is to say the enterprise must be identified, defined and qualified. This is essential for reaching a concrete understanding of the matters of concern to the investor and his motivations, both of which should throw light on his choice of strategies and on the flexibility of his attitude with respect to a given implantation.

On this basis it is possible to assess what is in fact the decisive role that may be played in the investing enterprise's strategy by considerations of the cost and productivity of the labour force available in the FEPZ and the relative importance of the other variables associated with the host country.

A. Investor qualification and motivations

1. Flexibility of implantation

The advantages offered to enterprises by FEPZs are obvious. In particular, the unique environment organised within the enclave provides them with an exceptional opportunity to test the climate in the host country at the lowest cost and within the shortest possible period of time.

Furthermore, for enterprises whose products have high specific value, FEPZs offer unrivalled scope for adjusting their production strategy to the multifarious market conditions and the requirements of the technology used.

The flexibility of enterprises in an FEPZ is all the greater insofar as their establishment involves a "light structure", i.e. a low level of fixed capital goods, as a result of the scale of diversified infrastructural facilities made available to investors by the FEPZ authorities and the virtual absence of formalities and red tape.

Accordingly, the enterprises concerned — which are incidentally known as "footloose industries" — can break off their activity and repatriate at any time, since FEPZ legislation is very permissive in this respect providing the minimum obligations are met. This usually means giving official notification of the cessation of activities, regularising their position with regard to employees, the tax authorities, etc.

Thus, production is reorganised by splitting the production processes into a series of technically feasible operations and by dispersing these operations geographically, hence relocating production.

The resultant segmentation of the production chain may affect different stages of the production process, each of which would be established at one or more particularly appropriate locations, each characterised by a specific mix of various inputs and production requirements such as low-cost labour, the proximity of major markets, and also the political and social stability of the host country, etc.

The process described seems to suggest that the phenomenon of relocation with a view to achieving export aims is encountered essentially among major MNES. An enquiry carried out among French investors in FEPZs showed paradoxically that small and medium-sized enterprises were in fact very dynamic.

In fact, as seems to have been established in the case of some Japanese enterprise located at Masan in South Korea[2], the subsidiary often becomes larger than the parent company. It is quite conceivable that many small and medium-sized enterprises, more exposed to international competition than larger ones, may have no other choice than to redeploy towards low-wage countries, and particularly their FEPZs which in addition offer their own specific exemptions and physical and administrative infrastructures that should help to reduce the investor's establishment costs to the strict minimum. Table 2 provides some data on the situation prevailing in South Korea in this respect.

Table 2. DISTRIBUTION OF PROJECTS BY VOLUME OF INVESTMENT (1980)

FEPZs South Korea

Unit : US$1,000

	Less than 300	Less than 500	Less than 1 000	Over 1 000	Total
Masan	29	11	19	30	89
Iri	4	4	2	2	12
Total	33	15	21	32	101
%	(32.7 %)	(14.8 %)	(20.8 %)	(31.7 %)	

Source. Data collected within the framework of the Development Centre's project.

The data in table 3 provide some guide to the average size of enterprises in a few FEPZs, although it is recognised that the number of jobs per enterprise is a very inadequate indicator.

2. Labour costs : a decisive factor

The quest for lower labour costs than those prevailing in the country of origin would seem to be a major reason why enterprises set up operations abroad, and this issue has

Table 3.   AVERAGE NUMBER OF JOBS PER ENTERPRISE
IN A FEW FEPZs (1980)

Country	FEPZ	Average number of jobs per enterprise
India	Kandla	67
	Santa Cruz	73
Egypt[1]	Port Said	
	Nasr	102
	Suez	
Mauritius[2]	Export-oriented enterprises	80
Mexico	"Maquiladoras"	193
Korea	Masan	333
Philippines	Bataan	367

Source : Data collected within the framework of the Development Centre's research project.
1.   Enterprises operating exclusively in the industrial sector.
2.   French enterprises only.

become particularly marked as a result of developments in this connection in most industrialised countries.

In 1980 the International Chamber of Commerce and the IFO Institute conducted a survey of 950 enterprises located in 45 countries which showed that higher wage costs had made a substantial contribution to the increase in the enterprises' costs in 80 per cent of cases and had been the major factor in 35 per cent of cases[3]. It would not therefore be surprising if the character of the labour force was a decisive factor in the decentralisation of highly labour-intensive activities and the most important criterion in the choice of a given site or FEPZ.

Such an observation relegates to second position the impact of the financial and tax incentives or the various grants which many FEPZs offer as part of their policy to attract foreign investment to their territory. Such a policy would at most influence the choice of the country of location, an observation that is based on the survey of FEPZs conducted by researchers at the Institut de l'Entreprise and IEDES[4] and corroborates the conclusions of many studies carried out in the broader context of the investment climate in developing countries.

However that may be, the findings of studies in this field concur sufficiently to allow us to consider it an established fact that labour costs play a fundamental and decisive role in any policy for the redeployment of industrial activities to FEPZs.

It should be pointed out, however, that the maintenance of employment within the enterprise in the country of origin is a matter of major concern to management. Highly sensitive to the attitudes of the trade unions, management usually seeks a consensus with employees on the need to set up in the host country.

These considerations, which weigh heavily in decision-making, may mean that the scale of activity abroad is determined in the light of cost equalisation within the enterprise so as to bring down the average cost of the product to a level ensuring a rate of return considered normal for the enterprise. Thus, once this average cost is reached, the process of redeployment would be curbed, so that activities would remain in the country of origin even if the profit margins were narrower than might be obtained by producing abroad.

Table 4 provides some data on comparative levels and trends of wage costs in a number of industrialised countries, newly industrialising countries and developing countries[5]. Care must be shown in interpreting such rough indicators due to the disparate nature of the data, which meant that hourly wages had to be calculated from daily wages.

Table 4. COMPARATIVE WAGE COST TRENDS IN VARIOUS COUNTRIES (1980)

	Hourly remuneration (in US$)		Change in the exchange rate of the national currency against the US$
	1975	Mid-1979 [1]	
Some Industrialised countries			
United States	$6.36	$9.09	—
Canada	6.14	7.97	−12.9 %
Japan	3.05	5.58	+36.4 %
			−12.5
Belgium	6.44	11.30	+23.5 %
United Kingdom	3.27	5.46	−1.6 %
France	4.63	8.17	−0.5 %
Fed. Rep. of Germany	6.24	11.33	+32.5 %
Ireland	2.82	=	−13.6 %
Italy	4.65	7.38	−21.6 %
Netherlands	6.57	11.31	+23.9 %
Some Newly industrialising countries			
Spain	2.70	5.62	−13.2 %
Brazil	1.13	1.80	−68.6 %
Mexico	1.89	2.31	−45.3 %
Hong Kong	0.71	1.25	+0.7 %
South Korea	0.37	1.14	0.0 %
Taïwan	0.48	1.01	+5.4 %
Other developing countries			
Peru	0.78	0.64	n.a.
Egypt	0.23	0.37	n.a.
Sri-Lanka	0.20	0.15	n.a.
India	0.17	0.33	n.a.

1. Except for Peru (1980), Egypt (1977), Sri-Lanka (1980) and India (1978).
— Names of countries in italics are those covered by our study.
Sources :
— *US Bureau of Labor Statistics in "Citibank", November 1980 ;*
— *Labor Statistics Yearbook for 1981, ILO ;*
— *International Financial Statistics, March 1982, IFS ;*
— *UN Monthly Bulletin of Statistics, March 1982 ;*
— *Hong Kong Monthly Digest of Statistics, October 1981.*

B. Cost and productivity of the labour force

It is extremely difficult to obtain satisfactory data, i.e. findings which can be interpreted accurately in making international comparisons of labour costs[6]. Without examining all the difficulties involved and analysing their many causes, suffice it to draw attention to the shortcomings of the evaluation methodology owing to the wide-ranging variations in exchange rates in particular and also to the fact the efficiency or productivity of the labour force is deployed in an area external to the domestic economy, in production conditions determined by foreign enterprises.

It is therefore more relevant to consider the working conditions in FEPZs as described by the authorities of these zones or the managers of enterprises established in them. In this connection, mention may be made of the studies by J. Currie[7] and O. Kreye[8] as well as the works of the OECD Development Centre group of experts.

1. Multiple factors in labour costs

The findings can only be very approximate due to similar methodological difficulties : distortions attribuable to the fact that social security charges (usually 20 to 30 per cent of gross wages) may or may not be taken into account, reference to an average wage in some cases and a minimum wage in others, disparities due to the types of industries selected, sex discrimination, unequal social security charges, etc.

Nevertheless, the findings show such wide differences between countries that there can be no doubt as to the role that remuneration of the labour force can play in the choice of a location. According to J. Currie[9], United States wage costs in 1977 were 16 to 57 times higher than those in the countries concerned. However, given the nature of the activity to be undertaken in the host country, it is clear that the structure of comparative wage costs by category of worker — as shown in table 5 — rather than by non-differentiated averages has a much greater influence on the location of an enterprise in one or other of the countries offering potential sites.

Table 5. AVERAGE MONTHLY WAGES IN MID-1978

	Taïwan	Japan	Korea	Malaysia	Philippines	Singapore	Thailand
Engineer	100	443	178	154	53	229	122
Accountant	100	315	193	196	39	191	103
Production manager	100	341	143	144	68	166	91
Typist	100	410	172	72	39	114	83
Foreman	100	406	133	105	40	112	55
Skilled worker	100	695	190	108	48	123	51
Semi-skilled worker	100	819	270	112	60	115	66
Unskilled worker	100	750	157	90	56	109	54
Cleaner	100	458	173	68	49	90	64

Source : Battelle - IFO - "Strukturveränderungen der deutschen Wirtschaft" Länderstudie, Taïwan, 1979.

The consideration of comparative labour costs alone does not give an accurate reflection of all the advantages offered in FEPZs by this input. Further qualification is called for as regards the working conditions (particularly the conditions governing recruitment and laying-off, settlement of disputes, etc.), and the attitudes of workers and of trade unions where they exist.

For example, weekly hours of work — 48 in most cases with the possibility of extension to 60 — might be an important factor in the economic calculations of the foreign enterprise. Work rhythms themselves may be intensive and annual paid holidays can be reduced to 4 days in some cases. By and large, it can be estimated that about 2 400 hours are worked per year, or some 20 to 30 per cent more than in Western economies[10].

Similarly, since physical working conditions in the strict sense do not usually conform to pre-established standards of hygiene, health and safety[11], significant savings can be made by the investor who turns to sites where installation structures and work organisation are not very costly while, on the other hand, infrastructural facilities are highly developed.

Since the workers in most FEPZs are isolated, it is particularly difficult to organise them as a collective force. In many situations, moreover, where unionisation is not prohibited, any demonstration, strike or other movement likely to compromise or even influence the social climate and rhythm of production is sternly repressed.

While it may seem exaggerated to consider that the labour relations and that of general working conditions are fundamentally different inside and outside FEPZs, the fact is that foreign enterprises located in such zones make the most of a form of remuneration peculiar to them, at any rate in the Asian countries, insofar as it comprises a substantial variable component which by means of a system of bonuses, is related to the targets set by the enterprise and the worker's performance.

This system enables the enterprise to vary the volume of labour required in the light of changing prospects on export markets. Accordingly, not only does the enterprise have greater flexibility to adapt to the situation on the international market but, given the uncertain nature of the income provided, the labour force is induced to conform to a very strict working discipline[12].

Moreover, while it seems that rates of remuneration in FEPZs do not as a general rule differ from those in the domestic industrial sector, export-oriented foreign enterprises pay higher wages than local enterprises producing for the domestic market, the reason probably being bound up with the productivity of the local labour force when part of a foreign production system. For example, in 1979 and 1980 the wages paid in the Egyptian FEPZs were 41 per cent higher than those paid in the domestic manufacturing sector for equivalent jobs.

2. Different levels of labour productivity

The fact that wages are low in developing countries is often attributed to lower productivity, so the initial difference in labour costs between the investor's country of origin and the host country would be narrowed by lower productivity in the latter.

The inductive analyses carried out in this connection on foreign implantation in the FEPZs of developing countries would seem to reach different conclusions : it has been found that, in production units set up in peripheral countries that have attained a certain level of industrialisation — mainly the newly industrialising countries — labour productivity is comparable and sometimes even higher than in the advanced economies for the same labour-intensive technology and for certain types of activity, e.g. assembly.

For example, P.W. Bareersen[13] established that the productivity levels reached in the "maquiladoras" in Mexico's border zone with the United States range between 80 and 140 per cent of the levels recorded in comparable American production units.

O. Kreye[14] reports that United States and German enterprises in the textiles, clothing and electronic equipment industries, which had set up plants in the Malaysian FEPZs found that after a few months they obtained the same level of productivity per worker as in comparable production units located in the United States and the Federal Republic of Germany.

The main industries concerned with this question are textiles and clothing — which are highly labour-intensive despite recent changes — and those producing components and assembling finished products in the electronics sector. The electronics industry combines advanced technology with the use of an abundant unskilled labour force, at any rate at certain stages which call for mass production. In this connection it may be pointed out that the production costs of the electronics industry in the Santa Cruz FEPZ in India are 40 per cent lower than those of the same industry in the domestic economy. It can be assumed that such results are attributable to the higher productivity achieved by FEPZ enterprises.

The processes described are therefore evidence of automated production involving some high capital-intensive elements together with assembly operations performed by unskilled labour which, in view of the work concerned, can be trained very quickly.

Moreover, enterprises located in the FEPZs of developing countries have a technological advantage in certain situations due to better control of the production processes, at any rate when they have an abundant supply of labour available. This advantage is bound up with the size of the target export markets which are set in a world context and permit significant economies of scale.

The above considerations relevant to labour productivity in the FEPZs of developing countries should in no way call into question or minimize the role that we have already stressed is played by the "cost" of labour in the competitiveness of the industrial goods manufactured by the production units concerned, since particularly stringent working conditions can be a major asset to the enterprise, especially when this advantage is combined with large-scale production.

IV. HOST COUNTRY STRATEGIES

The strategies of the host country can be determined by analysing the various components which help to shape these strategies and are in fact the main instruments.

Some of these components are fundamental and therefore fully warrant separate analysis. We shall also examine others which are less central but may nonetheless have an appreciable influence on the capacity of FEPZs to attract foreign investment to a greater or lesser degree. Such components include both the incentives offered to the investing enterprise and the established constraints which limit its action and in some cases are even serious obstacles to its effectiveness [15].

A. Determination and realisation of basic factors

The general tendency is to measure the success of an FEPZ by its ability to attract foreign investment, and the studies undertaken to determine the objective requirements for its success focus for the most part on the comparative merits of the advantages offered to the investor in terms of location.

The advantages offered may of course be analysed in terms of costs. Such an approach is highly necessary, at least if an assessment can be made of the costs and benefits to the host country. It is at this last level of analysis, i.e. assessing the benefits derived by the host country, that the greatest difficulties arise. However, it is precisely this final stage which should enable the country concerned to predict the value of the FEPZ and therefore shape its policy in this connection.

The advantages offered by FEPZs may be classified according to whether they are natural advantages such as geographical location, acquired advantages such as efficient infrastructures, or investment incentives such as tax exemptions.

Other classifications are conceivable, such as a breakdown by economic, institutional and socio-political components, or a breakdown by structural and cyclical components.

Our approach is more empirical, its principal merit being that it is a more specific response to the problem raised, namely to contrast the FEPZ strategy with that of the foreign enterprise. It should nevertheless be pointed out that the enterprise setting up in an FEPZ, however marked the "enclave" character of the latter may be, invokes the socio-political and institutional system of the host country and all the attendant guarantees, while at the same time its activities are conditioned by a climate comprising many economic components.

1. Socio-political components

Surveys have shown that the potential investor attaches the utmost importance to the political stability of the host country, to the attitudes of its government and population as a whole, to a tradition of respect for international commitments and acceptance of international arbitration procedures [16].

Some countries with FEPZs have concluded bilateral agreements guaranteeing investment, a notable example being Sri Lanka which has signed such agreements with the United States, the Federal Republic of Germany and the United Kingdom. South Korea has also signed an agreement of this type with the United States through the agency of the Overseas Private Investment Corporation - OPIC. Several of these countries are also signatories to the 1965 Convention on the settlement of investment disputes between States, whereby any dispute between an investor and the zone authority is submitted to arbitration. This is particularly the case of Sri Lanka and South Korea.

The legal guarantees sought by the investor tend to be more numerous and assume greater importance if the host country has not yet managed to establish a reputation for a favourable "climate" for foreign investment.

Moreover, legal guarantees themselves become pointless if the foreign investor has misgivings about the host country's economic system. The concern here is not so much the risk of nationalisation, expropriation or exchange controls as the need for assurance that the back-up services essential to the enterprises activities are efficient.

Such services include banking, sea transport, consultancy, legal and accounting services, telecommunications, etc., none of which can be improvised and all of which presuppose a certain business tradition which is not easy to find in countries where State control is highly developed, irrespective of the efforts made by the governments of such countries. Syria (Damas and Tartous zones) [17] is a cogent example. However, the linking of the FEPZ in other countries with offshore financial centres and free trade zones seems to have had a very positive impact, an example being the measures adopted by Sri Lanka to encourage the establishment of foreign banks so as to enable enterprises in FEPZs to have access to sources of international finance.

2. Organisation of international economic relations

In practice, the creation of a favourable "climate" for investment calls for considerably more than the provision of services and so requires an active policy with respect to international economic relations.

a) Trade relations

The trade agreements between developing countries and industrialised countries are an example of such relations. The customs exemption characteristic of FEPZs is meaningful only insofar as the finished products exported from these zones enjoy the preferential tariff treatment accorded to developing countries by the advanced economies, whether under regional agreements − such as the Lomé Convention − or in the context of "generalised preferences". However, as in the case of the Lomé Convention, most conventions lay down very strict rules of origin stipulating, in particular, that substantial processing of the product is required for it to be regarded as originating in the country concerned.

For example, products of assembly industries − precisely the type of industry frequently found in FEPZs − are excluded from the Generalised System of Preferences which is subscribed to by the United States, Canada, Austria, New Zealand, Japan, EEC Member States, Sweden, Norway, Finland and Switzerland.

Similarly, in the context of the Arab Common Market, the value added to a product must be 40 per cent of its total value if it is to benefit from preferential treatment. Moreover, the FEPZ should not be dissociated from the host country party to the agreement and on whose territory the zone is located.

Furthermore, each of the countries concerned has its own regulations on the matter and its own trade policy. Mention may be made of the special relationship maintained with the United States by Puerto Rico, and since 1975 by Liberia, and the agreements which link the EEC with Jordan, Egypt, Syria and to a lesser degree Sri Lanka.

All these initiatives, can enhance the value of locating enterprises in a given FEPZ, probably in a country whose trade policy has secured tariff concessions from an advanced economy or whose products have access to major markets by virtue of its membership of a regional group.

b) Tax conventions

There is also the example of tax conventions which are acknowledged to be useful when there is conflict, or at least lack of harmony between the basic principles governing tax legislation — the principle of personality and the principle of territoriality of the tax. Nothing will have been gained from the very substantial tax advantages granted to a subsidiary in an FEPZ if the additional profits corresponding to the exemption have to be paid over as tax in the country of origin where the parent company is located. This would simply mean that the developing country to which the FEPZ belongs has transferred tax revenue to an advanced economy, i.e. the investor's country of origin.

Given this situation it may be feared that the enterprises concerned will adopt, insofar as their "multinational" character allows, a "transfer price" policy which, being "profitable" from the tax standpoint, would tend to mask the economic reality regarding their location in the FEPZ.

In any event, the tax incentive system would break down and the enterprise concerned would either tend to restrict its activity or transfer all or part of this activity to a more advantageous location.

Many countries with FEPZs are aware of the importance of the issues and have signed double taxation agreements with the countries in which the investment originates. Such is the case in particular for Sri Lanka which has such agreements with Czechoslovakia, Denmark, Federal Republic of Germany, India, Japan, Malaysia, Norway, Pakistan, Sweden, Singapore and the United Kingdom.

3. The labour force

A number of developing countries have adopted an accomodating approach in taking measures to suspend labour and trade union regulations in the FEPZ with a view to providing an additional incentive to the potential investor. The main effect of such measures is to eliminate certain social costs and create a favourable "social" climate for industry.

In this connection it may be pointed out that there is no guaranteed minimum wage in South Korea and Malaysia in particular. Where such a wage is fixed, it is generally very low (for example, US$67 per month in Taiwan in 1980). There is also the question of the length of annual holidays — usually between 4 and 15 days.

Where legislation to protect the worker exists, it is in some cases circumvented by mutual agreement or is subject to special derogations. For example, the fact that there is an "apprentice" rate in Haiti means that so-called "apprentices" account for 30 to 40 per cent of the labour force employed in the assembly industries[18].

Where trade union activity is authorised, it is in most cases very limited due to the stringent legal provisions. In Singapore, for instance, where a single trade union is authorised, the 1968 Industrial Relations Act severely restricted its negotiating powers. In the Philippines, the right to strike has been suspended in what are regarded as "vital" sectors, while the FEPZ legislation in Mauritius prohibits trade union affiliation for five years.

In practice, it is not at all certain that such measures will really be to the investor's advantage in the long run. In fact in the case of a serious crisis the absence of institutionalised mechanisms for concertation may provoke a brutal rupture of social peace. Social insecurity and poor working conditions might lead to a fall in productivity and increased labour mobility, results that would seem to be all the more probable since the replenishment of the labour force might not always be assured.

It should be pointed out, however, that there is no apparent correlation between population size and the establishment of FEPZs and export industries[19]. Most of these zones are located in densely populated countries such as Mexico and Indonesia, but others are in countries with relatively small populations such as the West Indies and Haiti.

By and large, however, the countries which set up FEPZs are experiencing employment problems, as can be seen in the report by the International Labour Organisation[20].

Most FEPZs have a high rate of labour turnover, ranging from 5 to 10 per cent per month, primarily owing to the substantial labour reserves which include a very large proportion of women. It is estimated that women account for about 70 per cent of the labour force employed in FEPZs : 77 per cent in Masan, 87 per cent in Sri Lanka, 72.14 per cent in Malaysia and 70 per cent in Mexico. Female labour is usually preferred to male labour — available in most cases — for relatively unskilled jobs, not only for reasons of dexterity and discipline but also because the rates of remuneration are often 50 per cent lower, as indicated in table 6 giving data on the situation in Masan.

Table 6.   AVERAGE MONTH WAGES IN MASAN IN US$

Year	1974	1975	1976	1977	1978	1979
Men	99	139	165	213	274	322
Women	45	64	79	98	111	135
Average	59	82	99	127	151	182
Percentage rate of increase		39	20	28	19	30

Source : UNIDO, 1980.

It should be noted however that, as the FEPZs develop, the proportion of the female population in the total labour force employed tends to diminish significantly. For example, in the Malaysian zones it fell from 87 per cent in 1972 to 72 per cent in 1976 whereas the number of male workers doubled.

The same trend is observed in Masan where the proportion of the female population in the total labour force dropped from 90 per cent in 1971 to 75 per cent in 1979.

This trend is linked with a demand for increasingly skilled labour combined with the use of more capital intensive inputs.

Table 7 very clearly shows the relationship between the male/female labour force employed and the level of qualification required.

Table 7. PERCENTAGE BREAKDOWN OF WORKERS IN THE MASAN FEPZ
BY QUALIFICATION AND BY SEX

Percentages

	Men	Women	Total
Office workers and other clerical	5.2	3.5	8.7
Engineers	1.2	0	1.2
Technicians	1.3	0	1.3
Specialised workers	2.0	3.5	5.5
Semi-skilled workers	3.8	24.1	27.9
Apprentices	9.5	45.9	55.4
Total	23.0	77.0	100.0

Source : Data collected within the framework of the study (1981). Development Centre's research project.

The same pattern is seen in the FEPZs of Sri Lanka, showing the large proportion of male workers in the more advanced sectors which call for higher levels of qualification.

4.   The cost of transport

It would also seem that the cost of transport plays a major role in industrial location.

This factor is clearly linked to distance and it would be quite normal for FEPZs located in Central America and the Caribbean to produce mainly for the United States market, Mauritius for Europe, and Masan in South Korea for Japan.

In most cases, however, there are other more decisive factors such as loading and unloading costs in certain ports, to which must be added charges entailed by delays caused by traffic congestion. Account must also be taken of the problem of return freight which can very considerably increase the cost of transport in some cases, so it is not surprising that the cost of transport from Africa to Europe is sometimes appreciably higher than that from the Far East to Europe.

Such considerations can have a serious impact on an FEPZ's prospects in some cases. For example, the varied fortunes of the Kandla zone in India may be attributed to light port traffic which in fact goes mainly through Bombay, whereas the reason for locating the FEPZ at Kandla — a small port to the north of Bombay — was to relieve the latter of congestion and provide an alternative to Karachi.

The Malaysian authorities, realising the importance of transport infrastrures in determining the activities of an industrial zone, took care to ensure that all the FEPZs on their territory are located near urban centres with good transport services.

Logically, the cost of storage should be included in transport costs, particularly for air transport. Storage costs can be prohibitive in countries with poor transport services. Unfortunately, this cost is not published with the freight rates for the various destinations : comparative data need to be compiled.

In view of the foregoing considerations — which bring us to the question of infrastructures — the Indian authorities decided that enterprises in the Kandla FEPZ would be given a transport subsidy equivalent to 20 per cent of the f.o.b. value of exported products.

5. Infrastructures

The effectiveness of physical and administrative infrastructures is often a sine qua non for a given location in view of their decisive influence on "profitability" of implantation.

a) Physical infrastructures

Particular mention should be made of energy and water supplies and the quality of the communications networks, as it is important that the latter should have international links. It has been established that the FEPZs of Buenaventura in Colombia and Santo Tomas de Castillo in Guatemala were severely handicapped by poor communications systems and locations that were not particularly advantageous. On the other hand, the Santa Cruz zone in India has been able to take full advantage of its proximity to Bombay airport, whereas the inadequacy of Kandla's port infrastructures obliged the industries to use Bombay's port facilities, thus entailing excessive additional transport and administrative costs.

In this respect the Bataan FEPZ has been at a serious disadvantage owing to the evident shortcomings of its infrastructures, at any rate given the non-central character of its regional context. Water and energy supplies are particularly inadequate. In addition, serious communications problems have arisen and account for the fact that activities in the zone have been very slow in getting under way. Rail links are very clearly inadequate and, since there is no deep-water jetty, vessels cannot enter the port and have to unload onto barges.

The authorities of the Philippines took these facts into account when setting up two new FEPZs in 1979 (Mactan and Baguio). While, as in the case of Bataan, the two zones are in fact some distance from the huge conurbation of Manilla, they are nevertheless located in urban regions with good services, particularly where transport is concerned.

Although the FEPZs in Sri Lanka are located near Colombo, the country's main port, the latter's inadequate facilities and the consequent high port charges tend to be a serious disadvantage to the exporting enterprises established there. If the zones were well equipped with physical infrastructures, the volume of initial investment required by enterprises would fall considerably, industries would get under way more quickly and be able to get earlier returns on the capital tied up.

b) Administrative infrastructures

Administrative systems should be able to act efficiently and rapidly in applying the regulations : in terms of organisation, management and control : granting licences, concluding leases or contracts for the transfer of buildings, customs formalities, maintenance, etc.

The objective requirements for such an infrastructure have been analysed in detail elsewhere[21]. In any event, the body concerned has to have independent authority, especially as provision normally has to be made for back-up services in some cases and, more importantly, solutions have to be found for specific problems in a dynamic perspective ; for instance, the condition of physical infrastructures, the budgetary situation, the information and promotion campaigns, etc.

The Masan FEPZ may serve by way of illustration. The zone authority has very wide powers, since it even gives the necessary authorisation of foreign investment, and supervises the very wide range of back-up services for enterprises, primarily banking, insurance, catering, transport, storage and packing facilities and many other services. The

Sri Lankan authorities concerned even carry out promotion activities abroad, mainly in the countries of origin of investment. For example, seminars have been organised in the United States, the United Kingdom, the Federal Republic of Germany and France.

A comparative study of various forms of administrative organisation and procedures would certainly enable some conclusions to be drawn as to their respective efficiency and would clarify the options, since the problems arising in the various FEPZs throughout the world are sufficiently comparable for the exercise to lead to conclusions which can be applied on a general basis.

V. INCENTIVES AND CONSTRAINTS

A. Incentive measures

It is an extremely complex matter to establish a policy of incentives and to assess it. Attemps have been made on these lines, primarily with the aim of finding the ideal balance between granting advantages regarded as adequate from the investor's point of view and minimising the cost in terms of revenue lost by the State or the zone authority.

This balance in fact remains theoretical unless each situation is considered separately. The work done in this connection by the UNIDO experts in Sri Lanka is especially cogent.

Accordingly, we consider that transpositions from one situation to another would be particularly sterile. The effectiveness of incentive measures in the case of a given FEPZ depends less on the competitive nature of incentive programmes adopted elsewhere than on the scale of the shortcomings to be offset at various levels, primarily as regards infrastructures or the skills of the labour force.

Some light may nonetheless be thrown on the comparative merits of different incentives.

1. Tax incentives

The exemption from tax of profits made by enterprises in FEPZs does not seem to be a major factor influencing the investor's decision. Such exemption is usually granted for a period of not more than 10 years, in most cases for 7 years and often for 5 years. Depending on the case, exemption is total or partial and may be combined with other incentives such as deferred or free depreciation, indefinite carry-forward of losses, deductions for ploughing back profits. Some of these measures are, incidentally, only of value when exemption is not total.

Zones which are generally acknowledged to be successful, such as the Santa Cruz zone in India, offer very limited tax advantages to the investor, which suggests that zones offering exemptions for an indefinite period such as Egypt, or up to 1999 such as Senegal, are depriving themselves of valuable revenue unnecessarily.

The following tax incentives are usually offered by FEPZs in addition to the exemption of necessary production inputs :

— Exemption from export duties and other taxes such as professional tax, property tax, city and regional taxes ;
— Exemption from income tax for foreign personnel employed in the FEPZ ;
— Partial or total exemption from the tax on profits for varying periods and under diverse conditions. For example, total exemption in Malaysia for two to five years for enterprises with "pioneer status". Total exemption in South Korea for the first five years and then a tax rate of 50 per cent for the next three years. In Taïwan the terms and conditions of exemption have varied according to the

37

sector since 1973, whereas in Sri Lanka total exemption is granted for a period of two to ten years as determined by the number of jobs created, inflows of foreign currency, technology introduced, etc.

In addition to the above measures, it is often possible to carry forward losses incurred during the tax exemption period to be set against subsequent taxable profits. Such is the case for the Bataan zone in the Philippines in particular. Free or accelerated depreciation is also authorised in many cases.

2. Financial incentives

The provision of finance at reduced rates of interest would seem to be a much more effective incentive than tax exemption, since enterprises in FEPZs finance a good part of their fixed assets by means of loans.

Relatively few zones offer facilities for obtaining finance. Some that do are Mauritius, Dakar, Kandla in India and Bataan. In many countries, enterprises have access to well-established capital and financial markets where loans can be contracted on reasonable terms from international sources. Such is the case for a number of Far Eastern countries in particular. Exporting enterprises can sometimes obtain preferential rates of interest to finance their exports. This is so in South Korea where the rate is 12 per cent, compared with 19.5 per cent on the commercial market.

In some cases where it is feared that limited local financial resources may be diverted from use in the domestic economy, steps are taken to avoid conflicts of interest by ensuring that financing networks linked with foreign banks are developed within the FEPZs. These are usually authorised to engage in off-shore operations and for the most part enjoy significant tax advantages.

In Sri Lanka, for instance, since the enterprises in the FEPZ cannot use the local market for financing their fixed capital investment, they turn to banks authorised to finance off-shore operations. Special permission has to be obtained from the authorities in order to obtain "circulating capital" on the local market.

As regards exchange control, most FEPZs permit the unlimited transfer of profits as from the first year of production and repatriation of the total initial investment after a relatively short period, about three years.

3. Other incentive measures

Other incentive measures are also used and differ widely from one zone to another. These involve capital grants whereby the host country covers part of the cost of the fixed assets in a project or the cost of manpower training in one way or another. In Bataan, for example, 50 per cent of the manpower training costs borne by enterprises are deductible from the basis of assessment for income tax.

With a view to encouraging transfers of technology, the FEPZ authorities themselves finance some of the equipment in a number of cases. In Singapore, where efforts are being made to attract advanced technology industries, the authorities subsidise manpower training.

Grants may also be made in the form of interest or rent subsidies or for specific marketing services, product development, etc., all activities which are considered to be of value in the national interest.

Investors are often given the opportunity to lease at a low price standard-type buildings which can be simply adapted to their requirements. The foregoing measures are too varied in character and at the same time too specific to enable us to make any appraisal of their respective effectiveness, since they can only be fully assessed in their particular context.

B. Constraints

The system of incentives and promotional measures exists in conjunction with a number of constraints imposed on the investor in an FEPZ. In principle these constraints at first sight seem severe from the standpoint of the enterprise, although exceptions are made and considerable tolerance is shown in applying them.

While the FEPZ authorities are generally empowered to approve the establishment of an applicant enterprise only on the basis of criteria enabling them to make a practical selection (origin of investment, sector of activity concerned, etc.), they adopt a lax attitude for the most part since the amount of choice allowed to them tends to be rather theoretical.

In some cases, however, criteria relate to objective obligations. In South Korea, for example, an initial investment of $50,000 is required, while in Dakar the enterprise must create at least 100 jobs for Senegalese workers in addition to putting up a minimum investment of 100 million CFA Frs.

1. Access to the domestic market for FEPZ production

In most cases, access to the host country's domestic market for FEPZ products is strictly regulated, the principle adopted being simply to ban them entirely.

A more liberal approach has been adopted in some countries, such as Senegal, Egypt, Columbia and Brazil, with a view to developing industrial infrastructures in particularly backward zones. In other cases, including that of Sri Lanka, it was decided that by-products could be sold on the domestic market but only up to the equivalent of 10 per cent of total output. An exception was made in the case of a glass manufacturer for whom the limit was raised to 50 per cent for finished products.

China, India, Korea, the Philippines and Vietnam also allow zone by-products to be sold on the domestic market up to varying levels. In 1980, 4.3 per cent of the Masan FEPZ's exports went to the domestic market, but none of the products concerned was already being manufactured in the domestic economy.

Moreoever, while the enterprises located in Egyptian FEPZs sell 85 per cent of their output on the domestic market, it should be pointed out that these zones are not strictly industrial and that commercial warehousing activities predominate.

In both Egypt — where the authorities can allow FEPZ industrial products to be sold on the domestic market — and India, serious arguments are advanced in favour of greater tolerance. In the first case, the arguments relate to both the strong pull of a domestic market with a large absorption capacity and to the Arab embargo on products manufactured in Egypt, which severely limits the country's industrial export prospects. It would seem that the latter argument will carry less weight in the coming years as the other Arab countries will probably adopt a more flexible attitude.

In the case of India the absolute ban on selling FEPZ products on the domestic market may have curbed foreign investment which would seem to have been drawn towards zones that are more attractive, primarily owing to cheaper labour. Moreover, it would be difficult for Indian manufactures to decide to produce only for international markets where prices are lower than on the domestic market and quality requirements are by and large much higher.

One solution that might be adopted in the future would be to allow some of the products manufactured in FEPZ to be sold on the domestic market provided that customs duties are paid on them.

The argument carries sufficient weight for foreign enterprises investing in the Mexican "maquiladoras" to inform the local authorities that the precondition for any change in their supply and sub-contracting policy is the opening of the Mexican market to their products, whereas the authorities themselves are primarily anxious to protect national industries serving the domestic market.

This situation contrasts with that in Brazil where the authorities have promoted the development of the Manaus FEPZ which is primarily engaged in importing from abroad and is in fact a supply centre serving a region.

On the assumption that FEPZ enterprises have access to the domestic market, there will tend to be two types of effect according to the case : restrictive effects owing primarily to lost opportunities for manufacturing in the domestic economy, or stimulating effects as a result of new opportunities in the domestic economy to process by-products from the zone. On the other hand, it would seem specious to suggest that increased competition would have a stimulating effect on domestic industry, because the advantages and incentives offered to industries located in the FEPZ are generally much greater than those provided for domestic industry.

2. Competition on foreign markets between FEPZ products and domestic products

On export markets, too, it may be feared that domestic products will meet stern competition from FEPZ products. This problem seems to arise more particularly in the textiles, clothing and footwear sectors and, to a lesser extent, in the electronics industry. The argument is clearly relevant insofar as Taiwan has not authorised the establishment of new clothing industries in the FEPZ since 1974. Sri Lanka has purely and simply banned clothing exports from FEPZ industries to the European Economic Community which has an import quota on clothing from that country. Moreoever, no new plants are authorised unless the enterprise can show beforehand that outlets exist for its products.

Generally speaking, however, the outlets for products of FEPZs in developing countries must be located mainly in the developed countries ; this seems confirmed by the specific nature of the products, which give some indication of their final destination : electronic components, high quality yarns, footwear, optical and precision instruments, etc.

3. Establishment of joint ventures

Real prospects for the promotion of domestic activities and inter-penetration of the two spheres of activity would doubtless be opened by the establishment of joint ventures in the FEPZ. Such enterprises might be set up on a mixed-economy basis, i.e. with government participation, and combine the resources of the industries of developed countries with the more modest resources of enterprises operating in the domestic economy.

Some FEPZs have taken steps to encourage the establishment of joint ventures, or even to make them compulsory in some cases. In Sri Lanka, for example, while subsidiaries which are 100 per cent foreign-owned may be authorised by law to set up in the zone, not one of them has in fact obtained such authorisation. Investment in the Katunayake FEPZ is 70 per cent foreign-owned and 24 of the 27 enterprises operating there are joint ventures.

In India, a country, nevertheless anxious to preserve a certain independence vis-à-vis the outside world, 100 per cent foreign-owned enterprises are allowed to set up in FEPZs provided they are in sectors which are in particular demand from the standpoint of technologies and marketing capacities. Joint ventures are in the large majority in the Kandla FEPZ and there is a large foreign holding in only 13 of the 52 enterprises operating in the zone. Moreoever, many of these enterprises have concluded technical co-operation agreements or marketing tie-ups with foreign enterprises, irrespective of whether a holding is taken in the company concerned.

In the Bataan FEPZ in the Philippines, however, the number of wholly foreign-owned enterprises is diminishing. As shown in table 8, while investment by such enterprises accounted for 66.7 per cent of total investment in the zone in 1975, it accounted for no more than 38 per cent in 1979.

Table 8.   BREAKDOWN OF INVESTMENT (NATIONAL OR FOREIGN ORIGIN)
IN THE BATAAN FEPZ, PHILIPPINES, 1975-1979

Ownership of capital	1975		1977		1979	
	Number	%	Number	%	Number	%
100 % Philippine	3	20	12	27.20	14	28
Joint ventures with Philippine partner	10	66.7	19	43.8	19	38
100 % foreign	2	13.3	13	29.55	17	34
Total	15	100.0	44	100.0	50	100

Sources :   Snow, Currie, EPZAA Annual Report - 1979.

In Masan in South Korea some 24.3 per cent of total invested capital is in joint ventures. It would seem that the share of Korean nationals, both individuals and corporate bodies, continue to increase, having risen from 6.7 per cent of total invested capital in 1977 to 11.3 per cent in 1979. Table 9 shows the origin and proportion of foreign investment in the Masan and Iri FEPZs.

Table 9.   NATIONAL ORIGIN OF FOREIGN CAPITAL INVESTED IN FEPZs IN SOUTH KOREA
DECEMBER 1980

	Masan FEPZ				Iri FEPZ				Total			
	Sub-total	Japan	USA	Other	Sub-total	Japan	USA	Other	Sub-total	Japan	USA	Other
Number of enterprises	89	78	9	2	12	10	1	1	100	88	10	3
									100 %	86.3 %	9.8 %	3.9 %
Investment (in $	114.1	103	9.3	1.8	5.4	4.6	0.3	0.5	119.5	107.6	9.6	2.3
									100 %	90 %	8 %	2 %

Source :   Data collected within the framework of the Development Centre's research project.

In some FEPZ, e.g. in Beirut, where most of the enterprises are joint ventures, the successes recorded would seem to be largely attributable to the adopted form of co-operation which in fact achieves a close association of complementary capabilities.

NOTES

1. See E. Jahan, C. Jedlicki, M. Lanzarotti and J. Masini : "La stratégie des investisseurs français face à la concurrence des pays à bas salaires", Ed. by the Centre Nord-Sud de l'Institut de l'Entreprise and the Institut d'Etude du Développement économique et social (IEDES), University of Paris-I, February, 1982. Published by "Institut de l'Entreprise - IEDES".

2. See AMPO : "Free Trade Zones and Industrialisation of Asia", Pacific - Asia Resources Center - Tokyo, p. 55.

3. See Axel J. Halbach : "Industrial Redeployment Tendencies and Opportunities in Germany", 1979.

4. See *Op. cit.* : E. Jahan, C. Jedlicki, M. Lanzarotti and J. Masini.

5. Names of countries in italics in the table are those covered by the OECD Development Centre's project.

6. See, inter alia, V. Andreff : "Firmes transnationales et nouvelle division internationale du travail", in Revue d'Économie Industrielle - No. 14, 1980.

7. In "Investment : The Growing Role of Export Processing Zones", EIU Special Report 1979.

8. In "World Market Industrialisation of Developing Countries : Free Production Zones and World Market Factories". The New International Division of Labour. Max Planck Institute, Starnberg, 1977.

9. In "Investment : The Growing Role of Export Processing Zones", EIU Special Report, 1979.

10. *Op. cit.*

11. See O. Kreye, *op. cit.*

12. See P. Tissier : "Les zones franches d'exportation dans quelques pays d'Asie" in "Critique de l'Économie Politique", No. 14, January-March 1981.

13. In "The Border Industrialisation Program of Mexico", Lexington University Press, 1971.

14. *Op. cit.* page 336.

15. See : "The effects of investment incentives and disincentives on the international investment process". OECD Committee on International Investment and Multinational Enterprises, May 1982.

16. Jose de la Torre : "Foreign Investment and Economic Development : Conflict and Negotiation", Journal of International Business Studies, Autumn 1981.

17. See Antoine E. Basile : "L'extension en Syrie des zones franches", in "Le Commerce du Levant", Beirut, July 1979.

18. See P. Tissier : "Conditions de travail et zones franches d'exportation dans quelques pays d'Asie", *op. cit.*

19. See O. Kreye, *op. cit.*

20. In "Employment, Growth and Basic Needs - A One-World Problem", ILO, Geneva, 1976.

21. See T. Kelleher : "Handbook on Export Free Zones" UNIDO, July 1976.

Part three

RECONCILIATION OF OBJECTIVES AND "BALANCED ARRANGEMENTS"

It would be short-sighted and extremely unrealistic to try to resolve the problem, when there is one, of reconciling the objectives of the host country and the investing enterprise by attempting to find a balance between the costs incurred and the benefits derived by each of the two parties concerned. To pose this problem in static terms would lead only to superficial solutions, of a precarious and hazardous nature which does not need to be stressed.

Any "balanced arrangement" must fit in with the line determined by the growth and development requirements not only of the FEPZ concerned, but of the whole economy to which it is attached. Such a perspective means going further than measuring and offsetting the stimulating effects on the one hand and the restrictive effects on the other. It leads to the consideration and evaluation of the contribution of the investing enterprise and the FEPZ to the host economy generally, through the dynamics of the international specialisation engendered and the comparative advantages obtained.

VI. STATIC APPROACH : "BRAKING" EFFECTS AND STIMULATING EFFECTS

The "enclave" nature of FEPZs has been stressed at length in all the economic literature on the subject, though without the actual possibility of "economic" as opposed to "institutional" or "legal" disenclavement having been examined, at least systematically.

Examination of this point means ipso facto considering the links which develop between the FEPZ and the domestic economy and appraising the nature, importance, forms and effects of these links. According to the case, there will be a tendency to give more emphasis to "braking" or to stimulating effects. Only an in-depth, in situ analysis would make it possible to apprehend all the aspects of the question and to weigh the different factors influencing the balance between the two types of effects.

There are several ways of approaching the question of comparing the costs with the benefits derived by the host country :

— From the narrow, accounting standpoint, in terms of expenditure (public investment in infrastructures and other construction, investment by domestic private entrepreneurs to build factories in the zone, exemption from taxes, residual value of land and buildings, etc.) and income (salaries paid, insurance, rent received, net income of zone authorities, taxes and duties paid, etc.). A balance sheet of this sort is generally relatively easy to draw up. Reference can in fact be made to certain studies actually carried out along these lines[1].

43

— From a more specifically economic standpoint, itself depending on the objectives aimed at when the zone concerned was set up. These objectives differ from one country to another. It is known, for example, that technology transfer in the field of electronics was the ultimate goal when setting up the Santa Cruz FEPZ in Bombay. In other cases the objective is infinitely less specific and more general, for example, regional development. This goal seems in fact to have inspired the creation of Manaus in Brazil, Bataan in the Philippines, Kandla in India, etc.

A. Evaluation of expected results

Whatever they may be, the different objectives nevertheless have a common core, at least as regards the advantages expected, i.e. positive effects on :
— The use of production factors and other domestic resources, in particular the labour force ;
— The balance of payments — capital movements and current payments in accordance with export flows ;
— The acquisition of skills and know-how and, more generally, technology transfer.

Many of these factors are not all quantifiable and only find their full expression when set in the context of the economy as a whole.

1. Employment

Achieving job creation goals seems to be the major concern in countries with FEPZs, except, perhaps, for India where in view of the magnitude of the unemployment problem the contribution of FEPZs can be only marginal. The case of Mexico on the other hand, where the legislator in 1965 defined the "maquiladora" system in the context of employment and industrialisation policy, is very significant in this regard.

The "maquiladora" is a sub-contracting company, specially designed for foreign industrialists, which enjoys freedom from customs duties. At first such firms could be set up only in the frontier zone, but this restriction was modified in 1970 and 1972. There was thus a switch from a "closed system" to an "open system", the firm being entirely free to set up anywhere in the country. The concept of the FEPZ thus became one of "status" rather than territory.

The institution of the "maquiladora" in fact covers two situations : that of established firms which supply the domestic market and whose excess production capacity could be oriented towards export activities, and that of foreign enterprises coming to set up. In both cases, the intention is to reduce unemployment which is particularly rife in the frontier area in the north of the country where the demographic growth rate is very high and the population doubles every ten years. It was in fact in order to avoid over-concentration of workers in the north that the "maquiladora" was freed from the obligation to be located in this area.

The activities which have proved to be the biggest creators of jobs are those connected with the manufacture of electrical and electronic components and equipment, followed by the textile industry. These two sectors alone account for 80 per cent of the total work-force, which amounted to 120 000 in 1980.

Table 10 shows the distribution of jobs by type of activity in the Mexican "maquiladoras".

Table 10.   DISTRIBUTION OF JOBS BY TYPE OF ACTIVITY IN THE MEXICAN MAQUILADORAS

May 1980

Sector	Total firms	Number of jobs	Number of jobs per firm
National total	620	119 546	193
Food products	12	1 393	116
Clothing and other textile products	117	17 570	150
Leather and footwear	21	1 787	85
Furniture and wood and metal accessories	59	3 230	55
Chemicals and pharmaceuticals	6	120	21
Vehicles and transport equipment	53	7 500	141
Non-electrical machinery and equipment	16	1 834	115
Electrical and electronic components and products	66	29 774	451
Electrical and electronic components and accessories	157	39 627	252
Sporting goods, games and toys	21	2 803	133
Other industries	61	7 852	129
Services	31	6 047	195

Source : Compiled from data in "Sria, de Programación y presupuesto". Dirección General de Estadisticas. Mexico.

The best examples of FEPZs, at least as regards job creation, are to be found in South East Asia, and more particularly South Korea and Taiwan where there are almost 88 000 workers, while the number of jobs created in all the FEPZs established in Malaysia was some 80 000 at about the same time i.e. 1980.

In the case of countries like Egypt, while the number of jobs created in FEPZs has remained extremely low — almost 5 400 in 1980 — the reason is no doubt the domination of trading operations. Commercial activities in FEPZs in fact tend to create far fewer jobs than activities of an industrial nature.

By and large, while the number of jobs created in FEPZs is far from negligible, it remains relatively insignificant compared with the total active population of the country engaged in industrial production. The results would no doubt be more meaningful if they took account of the number of jobs created indirectly owing to the stimulating effects on the local industrial environment through enterprises providing ancillary services. Table 11 shows the breakdown by sector of the Egyptian FEPZ labour force.

The estimates concerning jobs created indirectly lead to very different results. In Egypt, it could be said that the creation of each FEPZ job leads to the indirect creation of another job in the domestic economy. In Taiwan, on the other hand, according to data provided by the FEPZ administration only one job is created indirectly for every four jobs created in FEPZ.

The jobs created directly or indirectly are mainly in unskilled or semi-skilled occupations. Thus in the Masan FEPZ, although a model of its kind, 83 per cent of the workers are apprentices or semi-skilled workers and only 8 per cent are engineers or skilled technicians, most of them being in the electronics sector.

It has often been held that by mobilizing the labour force available in the host country for offshore activities, the investor is depriving the domestic economy of the host country of the benefit of its own labour force.

The fact is that the numbers employed in FEPZs have never been very great in relative terms. It is only in a few countries (see table 12), such as Taiwan, Malaysia, the Dominican

Table 11. BREAKDOWN OF WORKERS IN THE EGYPTIAN FEPZs BY SECTOR (MID-1980)

Sector	Number of projects	Employment		Egyptian employment		Foreign employment	
		Number	%	Number	%	Number	%
I. Industrial activitivies	30	3 061	57.1	2 962	57.5	99	46.0
Food, beverage and tobacco	4	582	10.7	576	11.2	6	2.8
Textiles and clothing	8	1 655	30.8	1 632	31.7	23	10.7
Non-metallic minerals	4	62	1.5	52	1.0	10	4.6
Chemicals	9	492	9.2	454	8.8	38	17.7
Metal products	4	117	2.2	98	1.9	19	8.8
Electrical and electronic products	–	–	–	–	–	–	–
Miscellaneous	1	153	2.7	150	2.9	3	1.4
II. Commercial and warehousing activities	152	2 071	38.6	1 957	38.0	114	53.1
III. Financial services	3	231	4.3	229	4.4	2	0.9
Total	185	5 363	100	5 148	100	215	100

Source : Data collected within the framework of the OECD Development Centre's research project.

Republic and Mauritius that the population employed in FEPZs has represented over 1 per cent of the total active population of the country concerned. In Mauritius it has exceptionaly reached almost 7 per cent.

Considering the number of workers in FEPZs in relation to the total labour force in manufacturing activity alone, the rate of job creation becomes more significant (see table 12) : 8.4 % in Malaysia, 4.7 % in Taiwan, 27.42 % in Mauritius, 10.68 % in the Dominican Republic.

The argument raised against the foreign investor would however become more pertinent if instead of considering the ratio between the FEPZ workforce and the total active population in the host country, only highly-skilled workers were considered.

2. Value added

While job creation objectives are the main concern of the authorities in the majority of FEPZs, other factors which contribute to the formation of "local" value added also have to be taken into consideration. These are :

— Local supply of components or raw materials ;
— Payments, including taxes and duties, made by enterprises to the authorities ;
— Sums paid by way of rental for occupying land or buildings and as recompense for various services ;
— A share of the profits in the case of joint ventures.

Certain host countries impose a minimum local value-added before giving their authorisation to an enterprise wishing to set up in an FEPZ. Thus, in India, this minimum is 30 per cent of the export value. By and large, and in the specific case of India, the minimum laid down has been substantially exceeded , and in the case of Kandla, though there have been wide fluctuations, the average over recent years has been almost 40 per cent in labour-intensive industries and 50 per cent in stainless steel products. Table 13 shows the value-added share of Kandla FEPZ exports.

46

Table 12. CONTRIBUTION OF SELECTED FEPZs IN TERMS OF EMPLOYMENT (1981)

Country	Total active population	Active population in the industrial sector		FEPZs considered	Number of jobs created in FEPZs	Employment as a percentage of total active population	FEPZ Employment as a percentage of total industrial sector employment
		Number	%				
South Korea	13 061 000	4 310 130	33	MASAN IRI	30 642	0.23	0.7
Philippines	16 648 112	2 463 920	14.8	BATAAN	24 974	1.5	1.01
Malaysia	4 789 000	962 589	20.1	PENANG KUALA LUMPUR MALACCA	80 920	1.69	8.4
Taiwan	6 300 000	1 701 000	27	KAOSCHIUNG NANTZE TANTZE	80 166	1.27	4.7
SriLanka	5 413 050	811 957	15	KATUNAYAKE	13 200	0.24	1.62
Mauritius	300 000	73 500	24.5	Enterprises with FEPZ status	20 151	6.72	27.42
Senegal	1 770 000	159 300	9	DAKAR	600	0.03	0.38
Egypt	9 600 000	2 496 000	26	Enterprises	3 061	0.03	0.12
Mexico	16 600 000	4 150 000	25	"Maquiladoras"	119 500	0.72	2.88
Brazil	34 100 000	6 820 000	20	MANAUS	46 500	0.68	0.68
Dominican Republic	1 200 000	192 000	16	LA ROMANA SANTIAGO SAN PEDRO DE MARCORIS	20 500	1.71	10.68
India	261 000 000	28 710 000	11	KANDLA SANTA CRUZ	6 000	0.002	0.02

Source : Table drawn up on the basis of data in "World Tables", World Bank, second edition 1980 as well as in documents provided by free zone administrations.

Table 13. TRENDS IN THE VALUE-ADDED SHARE OF EXPORTS[1]
FROM THE KANDLA FEPZ, INDIA

Million rupees

Year	No. of jobs	Exports	Imports	Value-added	Value-added as %age of exports
1966-1967	70	0.75	0.95	0.16	21.33
1967-1968	150	0.89	1.27	−0.38	négative
1968-1969	250	5.18	2.41	2.77	53.47
1969-1970	300	6.02	3.39	2.63	43.63
1970-1971	450	3.44	3.43	0.02	0.58
1971-1972	550	7.97	3.28	4.69	58.84
1972-1973	400	15.11	4.54	10.57	69.95
1973-1974	300	17.69	5.88	11.81	66.76
1974-1975	500	18.01	8.53	9.48	52.64
1975-1976	650	21.92	8.43	13.49	61.34
1976-1977	850	35.23	13.18	22.05	62.59
1977-1978	1 200	47.17	17.66	29.51	62.57
1978-1979	1 500	55.27	25.34	29.93	54.15
1979-1980	2 500	93.97	50.48	43.49	46.28

Source : Data collected in the framework of the Development Centre's research project.
1. Exports are valued FOB and imports CIF.

This level has also been reached by the Masan FEPZ as the result of a process of constant integration through substituting local raw materials and semi-finished products for imports. Between 1971 and 1979, local value added as a percentage of export value rose from 28 to 52 per cent and, over the same period, the foreign raw material share of export value fell from 64 to 46 per cent, while the local raw material share of value added rose from 6 to 47 per cent and that of wages paid fell by 66 per cent. In 1980, almost 35 per cent of the total consumption of light equipment and components by firms established in FEPZs was obtained locally from Korean firms, generally by sub-contracting. Table 14 shows trends in "local value added" and its structure in the Masan FEPZ.

The same trend has been observed in Malaysia. These levels are generally very much in contrast with those reached in the Sri Lanka FEPZs where local value-added tended to be only about 4 per cent of the total value of exports.

Despite the efforts made by the Mexican authorities, in particular from 1977 on, to bring about the spread of "maquiladoras" over the whole country so as to induce the firms concerned to increase their procurement of local raw materials and components, the results obtained have so far been modest. Between 1975 and 1980, local value-added certainly increased substantially, i.e. to 16 per cent of the value of exports, but its structure remained stable ; wages still account for the lion's share and amount to 25 per cent of the total value of output while the local materials share does not exceed 1 per cent.

The largest part of value added in the FEPZs of developing countries consists of wages paid, a fact, consistent with what was generally the main concern in setting up the zones, i.e. job creations. As for the other local resources used, they almost always consist mainly of raw materials.

The propensity of the FEPZ investor to use local inputs depends very much on the sector to which he belongs. Thus in the textile and clothing industries this propensity is very slight[2].

Frequently, and this is probably particularly true of the electronics industry as demonstrated by Singapore, the multinationals concerned are not inclined to promote the

Table 14.

Table 14. TRENDS IN "LOCAL VALUE ADDED" AND ITS STRUCTURE
IN THE MASAN FEPZ, SOUTH KOREA

US$ millions

		1971	1972	1973	1974	1975	1976
FEPZ Massan	Foreign exchange earnings (A) (1)	0.2	25.9	76.7	180.9	251.2	313.5
	Ratio (%)	22.2	36.8	43.9	49.2	51.8	52.2
Manufacturing sector	Foreign exchange earnings (B)	421	1 588	2 369	5 455	7 321	8 742
	Ratio (%)	45.9	55.8	52.8	60.8	64.1	64.4
	(A)/(B) (%)	0.05	1.6	3.2	3.3	3.4	3.6
	Domestic raw materials	15	11 203	30 315	88 893	108 773	147 654 (47.1 %)
Breakdown (US$ thousands)	Wages	157	8 420	20 772	40 083	49 851	65 520 (29.9 %)
	Rents	19	694	998	1 373	1 546	1 881 (0.6 %)
	Public and other Services	47	5 564	19 897	50 564	91 034	98 436 (31.4 %)

Source : Data collected within the framework of the Development Centre's research project.
1.   Foreign Exchange Earnings : this variable is obtained by taking the difference between FEPZ exports and imports. Exports (FOB) - Imports (CIF).

The amount of local value added varies according to product (in the clothing industry it is estimated at an average of 30 per cent for production with a low labour content and 40 per cent for the others).

development of direct links with the domestic economy of the host country. Not only is intra-firm supply of inputs held to be a guarantee of quality and exact compliance with standards, it also permits an advantageous transfer pricing policy : it has been established that in the Santa Cruz FEPZ in India, firms' contribution to domestic value added was inversely proportional to the rate of foreign participation in their capital.

Certain FEPZ authorities — and this is the case in Taiwan — have developed and applied a system to encourage firms to increase their purchases of raw materials and even plant from local suppliers.

3.   Exports

FEPZ export performance is certainly a relative indicator of the success achieved by these zones since they were set up to attract export industries.

In 1980, the export performance of the FEPZ represented 3.6 of the country's total exports (as against 0.1. in 1975) for Masan, almost 7.5 for the three FEPZs in Taiwan, almost 6.8 for Bataan and 0.3 per cent for the Indian FEPZ. Table 15 shows the FEPZ contribution to total manufacturing exports in South Korea, India, the Philippines and Taiwan.

These approximate results are to be interpreted in the light of the level of industrialisation reached by the host country, usually a low level favouring a high FEPZ export rate, as in the case of the Philippines. It is also necessary to take into account the

Table 15.   CONTRIBUTION OF FEPZs EXPORTS TO TOTAL MANUFACTURING EXPORTS
IN SELECTED COUNTRIES

PERCENTAGE

Year	South Korea[1] (Masan and Iri)	India[2] (Kandla and Santa Cruz)	Philippines[3] (Bataan)	Taïwan[4] (the 3 FEPZs)
1975	3.4	0.09	—	8.65
1976	4	0.13	4.8	8.28
1977	3.8	0.20	6.4	8.13
1978	4.1	0.30	7.2	7.39
1979	4.3	—	6.8	7.48
1980	3.9	—	—	—

Sources :   1, 2, 3   Data collected within the framework of the Development Centre's research project.
4. Cf. EPZ : Essential Statistics : in Kwei - Jean Wang : report presented at the Colombo Symposium on "The economic social and impact of FEPZ", April 1980.

present level of development of the FEPZ, as there are several stages, each characterised by a given rate of export expansion[3].

4.   Technology transfer

In addition to the fact that it is very difficult to evaluate technology transfer, in particular because of the many forms it takes[4], there is reason to be sceptical as to the effectiveness and significance of the transfer made within the FEPZ.

The main reason is the strong vertical integration of the production process in the export-oriented industries. This can only favour routine activities, often highly automated, as in the case of the electronic component industry, and hence offering little chance for improvement, calling on unskilled labour which can adapt to the jobs created after only a few days' training. What is more, the specialised nature of the tasks prevents any skills acquired, however slight, being of use in other sectors of production.

In fact if any technology transfer is to take place under the conditions assumed, it is mainly by means of quality control which calls for higher levels of skill : supervisors, foremen, production engineers, management staff, etc. Thus, even if local nationals are employed on these tasks, the transfer effects will never involve more than a limited number of people.

This, at any rate, is the situation which seems to prevail in the Masan FEPZ, where "technicians and skilled workers" represent only 3.8 per cent of the total work force, or almost 8 per cent if engineers are included. During the training courses organised by the parent companies, the Korean workers never master the technology of the production system, but only acquire the basic technical knowledge necessary for the operation of the production process. They subsequently form supervisory staff midway between the Korean process workers and the (generally Japanese) management.

The sector to which the firm under consideration belongs also has a considerable influence on the transfer of skills : while in Masan where the electronics and chemical industries predominate, 3 000 to 4 000 workers have received technical training, in the Iri FEPZ, where the main activities are the leather-working and clothing industries, skills are considerably less developed.

It seems in fact, as has been shown in Sri Lanka, that the employment objectives, which imply low capital intensity in the production process, and the objective of technology transfer, have conflicting requirements as to the production methods used. The case studies show that certain industries, such as construction materials, require substantial investment for each job created, while the situation is reversed in the leather industry which creates infinitely more jobs. Certain industries, such as printing, occupy an intermediate position and some create numerous job opportunities at a moderate investment cost. Such industries are clothing, food products, textiles, followed by others such as toy manufacture, etc.

By contrast, the industries most likely to bring a technology transfer are those producing capital goods and intermediate products : electrical equipment, industrial chemicals, metallurgy, rubber, etc. The investment required is very substantial and job opportunities are very limited. It also appears that because of the need for a high volume of plant and other imports, the foreign involvement is particularly high.

Thus, a certain industrial know-how may be transferred through a firm established in the FEPZ, but the domestic economy will not benefit unless there is a certain mobility of skilled labour in its favour. Observation shows first that, staff turnover, in fact very high, is mainly within the zone itself and second, that this turnover generally affects relatively unskilled female workers who retire young from the labour market. It is not impossible for the creation of the FEPZ to have a negative effect on the domestic economy to the extent that it draws off the available skilled labour.

Nevertheless, the FEPZ may, in certain cases, have a substantial "demonstration effect" both for the local labour force and for the relevant authorities in the domestic economy, and this can happen on several levels : discipline in production, respect of deadlines, striving for quality, spirit of enterprise and innovation. The technological, managerial and other practices employed in the investor's country of origin are demonstrated through the FEPZ.

We should also point out the efforts made by the domestic authorities. Here we can cite the activities of the Korean Labour Office which is developing a plan including the creation of training centres, technical schools, etc. In Taïwan, almost 50 technical co-operation agreements of an average duration of five years have been concluded with foreign enterprises by the industries established in FEPZs. In Bataan, a regional worker training centre was inaugurated in November 1979.

The case of Malaysia is particularly instructive from this standpoint as a survey has shown not only that the plant in FEPZ industries is much more sophisticated than that of firms in the domestic economy, but also that through attaching themselves to the semi-conductor industry, other sectors have been able to benefit from the skills deriving from this industry through the mobility of skilled labour, in particular managers and high-level technicians. Such developments obviously have an impact which may be important in a country with a serious shortage of skilled labour. Table 16 shows the trend of employment, according to skill, in the FEPZ of Penang State in Malaysia.

In addition, the "demonstration effect" exercised by industries within the zone on enterprises operating in the domestic economy may be a significant factor in stimulating local firms to look to foreign markets. The catalyst role played by the FEPZ in the rise of Irish industry is very instructive from this standpoint : in 1966, the firms established in FEPZ exported 30 per cent of Ireland's industrial production ; in 1972, they exported only 12.9 per cent, even though in absolute figures their exports had increased substantially.

It is difficult, if not impossible, to define all the stimulating vectors covered by the "demonstration effect". It nevertheless appears that "exemplarity" with regard to quality and "industrial discipline" in a context which while cosmopolitan remains strongly "controlled" by the authorities, at least in certain FEPZs, are determining factors in the effect described.

Table 16.   EMPLOYMENT IN PENANG STAGE FEPZs, 1974-77

Employment category	1974		1975		1976		1977	
	number Total	%	number Total	%	number Total	%	number Total	%
Managerial and professional	286	1.64	346	1.65	413	1.59	483	1.7
Executive and sub-professional	643	3.69	461	2.19	867	3.34	1 384	4.9
Clerical and technical	1 810	10.4	2 141	10.19	2 847	10.95	3 641	12.9
Sub-clerical and technical	2 030	11.66	852	4.06	1 673	6.44	x	
Direct labour	12 637	72.60	17 209	81.91	20 181	77.68	22 604	80.4
Total	17 406		21 009		25 979		28 112	

Source : Data collected within the framework of the Development Centre's research project.
Not available.

B.   Problems of maximising positive effects

The stimulating or "braking" effects caused by foreign investment in FEPZs on the structures of the domestic economy seem to depend on the nature and intensity of many factors of which it is possible to identify the most important.

1.   Different forms of implantation

The probability that stimulating effects will in fact be exerted by firms set up in FEPZs depends very much on the type of enterprise concerned. It is possible to distinguish several types of enterprise and a number of classification systems have been drawn up to this end, a particularly pertinent one being that of H. Perlmutter[5] who distinguishes between ethnocentric, polycentric and geocentric types of multinational. More schematically, two categories may be retained and this will suffice for the present analysis.

The first type is characterised by the establishment of a "production unit" set up as a subsidiary of a foreign firm and whose activities are mainly limited to comparatively simple assembly operations. The fairly unskilled workforce is mainly female, the raw materials are imported, the finished products are delivered to the parent company, etc. The management, made up of foreigners, is replaced by nationals usually only after a long period. In any event, the major decisions concerning management, marketing, the organisation of production, research and development activities, etc. are made by the parent company alone. The subsidiary thus has very little autonomy and consequently very few supervisory staff.

The extremely close and virtually exclusive links which the subsidiary has with the parent company obviously tend to limit considerably the possibilities for sustained relationships with firms located in the host country.

The second category of firm to establish itself in an FEPZ is characterised by the implantation of a completely integrated "production unit" in the form of a subsidiary company, some of whose capital may be contributed by a local enterprise or interest group. The subsidiary's activities extend to manufacturing operations and on this basis links are established with the domestic economy, implying stimulating effects. The labour force is more skilled than in the previous case and raw materials and semi-finished products are purchased locally. Furthermore, the management structure is much less "foreign" and includes many more locals. Finally, and above all, it enjoys very much more autonomy in running its affairs than is the case with the first category.

By and large, the economic structures of developing countries, which FEPZs cannot shed entirely, tend to favour the establishment of the first type of firm in their enclaves. There is nevertheless an admittedly slow move towards the second category.

2. A strategy subject to external requirements

A second qualification of the foreign investor's strategy is due to the fact that the subsidiary's dependence on the parent company is so strong that it is really subject to the policy constraints of the country of origin, as well as those of international markets, while being impervious to the influence of the host country and unaware of its needs. There has been a good deal of discussion about the "extraneousness"[6] of decision-making centres in the case of foreign enterprises established in FEPZs, the dependence which may result for the host country's economy and the destablization effects brought about by investment or disinvestment flows and the flows connected with actual operation. There is thus some reason to fear that the subsidiary may be an unstable employer whose decisions depend on events quite outside the host country.

The probability of such negative occurrences is all the greater since the enterprise is mainly concerned with finding locations providing security and specific favourable conditions, hence it needs to ensure maximum mobility.

The only safeguards the FEPZs might have against the effects of a shift of interest by multinationals would be efficient administration of the zone and diversification of investors by country of origin and, above all, by sector.

The second condition does not seem to be fulfilled in the majority of cases. One point is that the importance of "proximity to markets" in the location of firms tends significantly to influence the "nationality" — in the sense of country of origin — of the investor, at least in certain situations. Empirical research has in fact shown a strong concentration of Japanese and Australian investment in Asian FEPZs, while in Latin America the main source of FEPZ investment is the United States.

Another point is that the vertical integration of production in FEPZs and the nature of the advantages offered tend to encourage particular types of industrial activity (assembly or component manufacture), which are therefore common in the majority of FEPZs[7]. The possibilities for industrial diversification are therefore limited. The fact is that the structure of industrial activities in each FEPZ, as shown in table 17, depends very much on the stage of development of the FEPZ concerned. The examples of South Korea and Sri Lanka are significant in this respect[8].

It should be pointed out, however, that while in certain situations it has been possible to pursue the objective of diversifying activities within the FEPZ, as in the case of Kandla, other objectives incompatible with this may have been set for other FEPZs. Thus in India itself, the authorities plan to promote increasing specialisation of the Santa Cruz FEPZ in the manufacture of a specific type of electronic product. It should be pointed out that the firms in this FEPZ already export almost 16 per cent of all the electronic products produced in India for export.

3. Concrete possibilities of domestic sub-contracting

Apart from the supply of raw materials and a number of general services necessary for the operation of FEPZs — construction activities, energy supply, roads and other infrastructures — sub-contracting is an ideal way to break the "enclave" of the FEPZ and

Table 17. ENTERPRISES AND INVESTMENT BY SECTOR IN SOUTH KOREAN
AND SRI LANKA FEPZs 1980

Sector	Number of enterprises %		Investment made %	
	South Korea	Sri Lanka	South Korea	Sri Lanka
Electrical and electronic	27.5	7	46.7	14
Metallurgy	19.6	1	23.5	1
Precision	8.8	15	8.4	8
Textiles, clothing and footwear	14.7	42	7.4	29
Capital goods	4.9	0	2.5	0
Non-metallic products	2.9	18	0.7	17
Other products	21.6	17	10.8	41
Total	100	100	100	100

Source : Data collected within the framework of the Development Centre's research project.

penetrate the host country's economy and, obviously, increase local value-added. This is certainly a factor likely to modify the existing industrial structure, when there is one.

Using a typology of international sub-contracting ("ISC") proposed in a previous Development Centre study[9], it is possible to identify two types of ISC between enterprises within the zone acting as principals and local units operating as sub-contractors, according to whether the principals[10] are the subsidiaries of multinationals established in the zone or independent enterprises.

Although the majority of case studies show implicity that sub-contracting operations between the FEPZ and the domestic economy are not lacking and are even sought by the host country authorities, this situation is explicit only in three countries — Malaysia (for electronics firms in particular), South Korea and Sri Lanka. In the last two countries, the sub-contracting agreements cover a more varied range of manufactures. It should also be pointed out that while sub-contracting activities are expanding in Sri Lanka where FEPZs are still at the beginning of their "life cycle"[11], they are clearly declining in South Korea where FEPZs are reaching the end of their life cycle and being progressively absorbed into the domestic economy.

More generally, it appears that the development of sub-contracting activities depends on the environment in which the FEPZ concerned is situated. Thus the location of the Santa Cruz FEPZ in India and the Bataan FEPZ in the Philippines in relatively isolated areas characterised by a lack of industrial structures (particularly in the case of Bataan) is the main reason for the lack of links with the existing local industrial potential.

In addition, it may be that lower wages outside the FEPZ may favour sub-contracting activities, as is the case in South Korea.

It also seems that sub-contracting operations, in particular those covering the supply of semi-finished products, are related to the size of enterprises in the FEPZ, small and medium sized firms favouring the development of sub-contracting.

By contrast, large, highly-integrated multinationals tend to promote transactions within their own structure, the segmentation of production processes being accompagnied by a high proportion of "captive" trade.

It is very difficult to obtain precise and comparable data as to the size of firms in FEPZs though it is possible to determine orders of magnitude by referring, according to the case, either to the number of jobs created or to the amount of capital invested. Such information leads to the conclusion, for example, that in Kandla in India, small and medium-sized firms are dominant : in 1980, 37 out of 43 units represented investment of under 30 million rupees and the average number of workers per firm was 67.

In South Korea, the average size of units in FEPZs is larger. Thus of 101 projects approved at Masan and Iri, 31.7 per cent of investments were over US$ 1 million and in Masan the average number of workers per firm was 333 in 1980, which indicates quite a respectable size. By and large, the distribution of large and small units is fairly homogeneous.

As in the case of Masan where, in 1980, 35 per cent of FEPZ needs in light equipment and components were obtained locally, firms are thought to be turning towards sub-contracting, either to meet orders for which their production capacity is not great enough (capacity sub-contracting), or for labour cost considerations, the wages paid by sub-contractors being lower, as mentioned above.

In the case of Masan, 50 firms within the zone sub-contract to 130 local firms operating within the domestic economy and the sub-contracting agreements concluded often include technical assistance in order to obtain high enough quality to satisfy international standards. Thus, exports by firms within the zone include 24.2 per cent of domestic inputs obtained outside the zone. In addition, the law allows 40 per cent of the total production process to be carried out outside the zone. Table 18 gives some indication of the supply of raw materials to the Masan FEPZ for the period 1971 to 1980.

Table 18.   RAW MATERIALS SUPPLIES IN THE MASAN FEPZ, SOUTH KOREA

Year	FEPZ exports (A)	Local raw materials (B)	Foreign raw materials (C)	B/A	C/A
1971	857	15	550	1.8	64.2
1972	9 739	415	5 909	4.3	60.7
1973	70 734	11 203	37 327	15.8	52.8
1974	181 547	27 565	79 925	15.2	44.0
1975	174 803	30 315	92 315	17.3	52.7
1976	303 001	63 667	145 403	21.0	48.0
1977	367 918	88 893	177 277	24.2	48.2
1978	484 788	108 773	241 321	22.4	49.8
1979	600 558	144 300	283 003	24.0	47.1
1980	628 110	142 872	289 587	22.8	46.1
Annual Average 1971-1980	108.1	176.8	100.6	—	—
Growth rate 1975-1980	29.2	36.4	25.8	—	—

Source : Data collected with the framework of the Development Centre's research project.

In Penang, the share of inputs of domestic origin obtained outside the zone in the total output of the FEPZ grew substantially between 1973 and 1978 : from 1.6 to 12.8 per cent, as shown in table 19. The regular and strong increase in supplies of raw materials and components from firms operating within the domestic economy was in fact accompanied by a significant supply of capital goods from local firms, i.e. 20.7 per cent of the whole in 1979.

Table 19.   ORIGIN OF INPUTS USED BY FEPZ ENTERPRISES IN PENANG STATE, MALAYSIA, 1973-1978
M$ Thousands

Origin of raw materials and components	1973		1974		1975		1976		1978	
	Value	%	Value	%	Value	%	Value	%	Value	%
Foreign	132 863	94.4	311 216	96.86	294 354	90.16	572 377	92.29	844.178	87.1
Local	2 163	1.6	10 097	3.14	31 021	9.84	47 791	7.71	124 091	12.8
Total	135 026		321 313		315 375		620 168		968 269	

Origin of capital goods	Value	%	Value	%	Value	%	Value	%	Value	%
Foreign	32 847	87.99	131 548	73.8	71 049	52.07	24 194	84.16	27 727	79.34
Local	4 484	12.01	46 703	27.2	65 398	47.93	5 990	19.84	7 220	20.66
Total	37 331		178 251		136 447		30 184		34 947	

Sources : PDC Annual Reports Malaysia 1981.

56

4. Participation of local investors

While, as has been shown, a significant level of local participation is required in some cases by the host country authorities, in other situations, particularly if the FEPZ concerned is successful, such investment takes place spontaneously. This is the case of Shannon, where the proportion of firms 100 per cent locally owned is increasing, and was also the case in the Beirut FEPZ. In both cases, however, the initial economic and industrial environment was relatively well-developed.

In South Korea, too, where the Masan and Iri FEPZs are considered exemplary, wholly foreign FEPZ investment in 1980 amounted to US$86.4 million, or 75.7 per cent of the total, while joint investment at the same date amounted to US$27.7 million or 24.3 per cent of the total. Of a total of 101 projects, 37, or 36.6 per cent of the total were joint ventures in which the South Korean partner had a majority holding in 60 per cent of cases.

The issue raised in Part Two concerning the catalyst role of the joint venture, largely explains the trend towards increased participation of local capital in FEPZ firms, and sometimes even its preponderance.

5. Joint use of existing potential and the "size effect"

FEPZ activities and industrial activities in the domestic economy, as well as other related activities, can in certain cases be combined so as to reach such a size in the exercice of certain functions as to permit significant economies of scale, whether these be "internal" or "external" to the firm.

Joint use of existing facilities can be envisaged in particular in the case of infrastructures and certain services, in which a significant improvement can thus be expected.

These benefits can only be realised to the extent that the FEPZ concept becomes "institutional" rather than "territorial", the FEPZ then being defined by a "system". Firms enjoying "FEPZ status" can then be established anywhere in the country and can thus choose what they consider the most favourable location, given the constraints and restrictions imposed by the host country authorities. There are various types of administrative control over the firms concerned, which thus benefit from duty-free imports of materials to be re-exported in one form or another. The system in force may be "draw-back" or "manufacturing in bond".

FEPZ countries, which have turned towards such solutions include Mauritius, Singapore and Tunisia in respect of firms established under the 1972 Act on the Tunisian Investment Code.

In addition to the case of Mexico, whose unique "maquiladoras" system has already been described, we would point out the specific case of Sri Lanka where the FEPZ system has tended to spread over the whole country. In India too, the system governing firms operating in the Kandla FEPZ is tending to spread to all firms, whatever their location, whose production is destined exclusively for export markets. The facilities granted to these firms, in particular as regards liberalisation of imports, is tending significantly to reduce the specific attraction of FEPZs.

6. Incentive-induced "industrial" specialisation

Excessive advantages in the form of tax or financial incentives or connected with social legislation, etc., can bring about a reallocation of factors of production on the international level which is not in harmony or even compatible with the comparative advantage of the different trading partners. This could result in international specialisation involving a "wastage" of (already scarce) resources in the developing countries because of their below optimal allocation and could favour an uncompetitive structure of the economy.

As regards the wastage of host country resources corresponding to the incentives described, surveys carried out among investors have tended to show that while the decision to relocate is generally independent of incentive policies, the latter nevertheless have some influence on the choice of host country.

It is therefore not surprising that because of growing competition the countries concerned are moving towards extremely liberal investment codes. Furthermore, such developments obviously run counter to any effort which might be made in the direction of improving social legislation and working conditions generally. This problem was raised at the UNIDO Conference in Barranquilla in 1974. It was suggested by the experts present that there should be agreements on the maximum level of concessions granted to foreign investors by FEPZs, at least those within the same regional group, but this idea was not followed up.

On another level, but along the same general lines, we might mention a draft code of conduct presented to the World Export Processing Zones Association. This includes in particular the obligation on FEPZs to grant import authorisations only to investors who undertake not to impose any restraint on wage increases, to the extent that these would permit an equal level of remuneration to that prevailing in the domestic economy of the host country. This code also provides that the labour legislation in force throughout the host country should also extend to FEPZs and that trade unions should be able to operate freely in such zones.

As for the industrial specialisation resulting from the incentives described, to the extent that it can be qualified as such, it would not reflect a high level of economic development any more than it would correspond to a deliberate policy expressed through a national development plan. This would be the case, at least, as long as the incentive policy pursued was not based on the "real" advantages obtained in the host country.

Furthermore, a vertically integrated export-oriented multinational industrial enterprise would tend to develop highly compartmentalised specialisations in the different countries to which it extends its activities, thus encouraging an international division of labour which is not necessarily to the advantage of the countries concerned[12], which will find themselves trapped in their initial specialisation with their chances of advancing to more sophisticated production irretrievably harmed.

The research carried out does in fact seem to suggest the predominance in FEPZs of industrial "mono-structures" characterised by lack of complexity in the manufacturing processes used : textiles, yarns, metal products, electrical goods, optical instruments, toys, etc. — products closely associated with the consumer goods industry[13]. Such industries are often based on highly labour-intensive manufacturing processes, the main advantage for the investor being rapid depreciation and obsolescence of equipment.

It follows that the foreign trade of the host countries concerned does not depend solely on their factor endowment, but also to a large extent — sometimes almost entirely — on the changes in their comparative advantage brought about by the economic policy pursued by their governments and the strategies of multinationals.

VII. DYNAMICS OF SPECIALISATION AND ACQUIRED ADVANTAGES

The constantly evolving pattern of international economic relations makes it impossible to consider any comparative advantage as being definitely acquired or assured of survival. The possibility of maintaining the advantage is also conditioned by the changes introduced by technology in general as regards both the product and the processes which go into its making.

There are therefore two alternatives of which the first is to rise in the hierarchy of international specialisation by means of learning "sequences" which imply the mobilisation and effective contribution of the whole national economic potential of the country concerned ; this should be done in conjunction with the implementation of a differentiated and constantly adjusted policy on direct foreign investment. The other alternative amounts to a laxist attitude which can only lead to outright regression.

It becomes thus imperative for the FEPZs themselves to evolve in consequence, thus reflecting a degree of correspondence with the host country's economic situation at a given moment.

More generally, it might be possible to identify trends and orientations of policies to attract export-oriented investment capable of promoting the economic structures felt to be desirable.

A. Comparative advantage and change factors

The concept of comparative advantage is relative. The relocation phenomenon clearly illustrates this relativity, the enterprise being permanently in search of the most suitable location in the world in which to establish, but with no assurance the location chosen will continue to be the best choice.

The attraction to firms of an FEPZ location enabling them to make the most of a plentiful supply of cheap labour has been abundantly stressed.

How permanent such an advantage is depends on the extent to which the FEPZ can ensure the maintenance and review of identical conditions for mobilising labour. This in turn is related to wage-structure changes and the industrial policy pursued in the host country at least insofar as it affects the FEPZ.

Wages can be expected to increase at least in nominal terms under increased demand pressure due to the inflow of foreign capital. This increase, as is the case in South Korea, is less marked in the FEPZs than in the domestic economies but it remains strongly influenced by general developments affecting the economy as a whole.

In Masan in 1971, at the time when the FEPZ was created there, the average wage was distinctly higher than the prevailing level for the domestic economy, but the trend towards equalisation led to roughly equivalent wage-levels in 1980.

Nevertheless the developments described are governed in essence by the industrial policies followed.

Thus, in Singapore the Government took the initiative of substantially raising wages, and the authorities in South Korea made appreciable concessions with regard to wage rises : the manual worker's wage in that country increased by 22 per cent between 1979 and 1980. In fact, the measures described — which point to a labour shortage — tend to be used not so much as an instrument of social policy but far more as an incentive to use more technology-intensive production processes which employ a more skilled labour force.

The policies resorted to seek mainly to achieve upstream industrial integration while maintaining continued expansion of exports. South Korea provides a particularly striking illustration of this : the country began by manufacturing synthetic fibres and in a second stage went on to create petrochemical complexes. Nowadays, it not only manufactures textile machinery but even exports turn key plants [14]. Table 20 shows the way in which the fundamental objectives, development strategies and growth industries have evolved and so contributed to economic progress in South Korea.

Table 20. PROGRESS OF KOREA'S ECONOMIC DEVELOPMENT

	1st Plan 1963-1966	2nd Plan 1967-1971	3rd Plan 1972-1975	4th Plan 1977-1981
Fundamental objectives	The development era begins and institutional structures are set up.	High growth and rapid industrialisation.	Improved industrial structure, stable and harmonious growth.	Sustained growth and social development
Development strategy	Reduction of main bottlenecks : — investment in infra-structure ; — development of basic industries ; — local goods substituted for imported consumer goods.	Export-oriented industrialisation : — increased exports of consumer goods ; — local products substituted for imported consumer and intermediate goods ; — infrastructural expansion.	Growth, stability and equilibrium : — development of the rural economy ; — development of heavy chemical industries ; — exports of intermediate and capital goods begin	Growth harmonization. Efficiency and greater equity : — strengthening of self-reliant economic structure ; — development of industries making intensive use of technology and skilled labour ; — improved international competitiveness through increased efficiency and technological innovation ; — promotion of social development and greater social justice increased ; — exports of capital goods
Growth industries	Electrical energy ; fertilizers ; textiles ; cement.	Synthetic fibres ; petro-chemicals ; electrical equipment.	Iron and steel ; transport equipment ; electrical appliances ; shipbuilding	Iron and steel ; machinery ; electrical equipment ; shipbuilding components.

Source : Korea Business No. 4 - 1976, A18.

Change on this scale is bound to involve some development in the skill levels of the labour force, since the new activities call for ever more advanced technology, in combination with capital-intensive means of production. The same trend is observable in Taiwan. It leads to a frequently drastic conversion of the FEPZ, involving changes in conditions of employment and secondly a deliberate move towards specialisation in activities with a high technology content.

Hence, amongst the proliferation of FEPZs, categories can be discerned each of which corresponds to a specific phase in the development process described. On this basis, types of specialisation might be identified which however can be considered and interpreted only in a resolutely dynamic perspective.

The life of the FEPZ would thus follow a succession of cycles in which successive kinds of specialisation are acquired in turn, with each cycle comprising the following phases :

— In the first phase the FEPZ is provided with basic infrastructures and appropriate facilities. This phase is characterised by significant foreign investment flows.

- In the second phase of expansion the foreign investment flows continue to increase in absolute terms, but decline in relative terms. Exports expand strongly while the FEPZs occupancy rate reaches its maximum.
- The third phase is that of maturity. While the foreign investment flows tend to level off, exports increase at a slower rate than before and small marginal businesses tend to be replaced by larger enterprises employing staff with better technical training.
- The characteristic feature of the fourth and final phase is disinvestment by the foreign enterprises whose assets are as a rule taken over by local interests.

The end of this final phase should mark either the start of a new cycle in which the FEPZ turns towards more sophisticated manufactures, or the beginning of the phasing out process as the zone has become superfluous with the creation of industrial structures capable of developing independently.

This second possibility leads on to the more general question of the relationships that may exist between the life cycles of FEPZs and the development cycle of the country in which they are established. Thus changes in conditions in the host country will affect the manner in which that country's authorities perceive the role of the FEPZs, independently of their age. For example, insofar as employment ceases to be the primary objective, the zone might play an important role in attracting foreign investment involving high value added. This would no longer mean a decline in investment in the FEPZ as it "matures", but simply a change in the zone's industrial structures accompanied by new partners, in conformity with the pace and objectives of development in the host economy.

B. Future trends and orientations

One should stress the part that can be played by the authorities of the country concerned in the incentives described and the changes which could lead the FEPZ to a specialisation better adjusted to the requirements of industrialisation and likely to provide the best response to the changing and multifarious needs of international investment.

This might be one condition for the permanency of FEPZs which would in practice involve the establishment of firms that would engage in new higher technology, capital intensive activities and through greater vertical integration, would help to make value added locally more substantial.

The host country authorities might even promote a new type of FEPZ as in the case of Taiwan. The "industrial and scientific complex" launched in 1979 near Taipei at Hsin-Chu, comprises a number of training institutes and research laboratories. As early as 1980, approval was given to five American projects. Two of them will produce integrated circuits, two computers, and the last will specialise in the manufacture of laser optical instruments.

The advantage to the foreign investor is that highly-skilled, high-level technical and managerial staff is available on the spot at distinctly lower levels of pay than those of their Western or Japanese counterparts.

Other measures may be deployed such as creating advanced training centres. This was the scheme that the authorities of the Bataan FEPZ decided to undertake in November 1979.

The tensions developing in the advanced economies as a result of the deep and lasting recession have led to a number of pressure-groups adopting a negative attitude towards the semi-industrialised countries, and hence towards the institution of the FEPZ. This attitude is reflected in the upsurge of protectionism. The goods most affected are textiles, shoes, leather and leather products and more recently, certain electrical and electronic equipment, toys, etc.

The countries affected are those whose industrial production is highly competitive. Thus, FEPZs in the following countries are particularly concerned : Taiwan, South Korea and Mexico.

The argument of protecting industries — and hence employment — in the countries of origin is not convincing. A survey amongst a few industries in France arrived at the conclusion that in general, for firms with an establishment abroad, redeployment had not caused loss of jobs ; for a number of them, on the contrary, it was cost-sharing between manufacturing in France and abroad which enable them to stay in business and thus helped to maintain numbers employed in the country of origin[15].

Developments of this kind, together with observed trends in wage-structure and industrialisation policy in the newly industrialising countries, can only precipitate the emergence of the second generation of FEPZs. Thus, enterprises are tending to turn away from FEPZs in Taiwan, South Korea and Singapore to those in the Philippines, Malaysia, Sri Lanka, Haiti and recently China where four FEPZs are in process of installation and will supply a large body of unskilled labour.

Moreoever, new FEPZ investors are making their appearance, this time Asian multinational enterprises, generally on a small scale. They are from countries with first-generation FEPZs such are Singapore, Hong Kong or Taiwan, and are establishing in second-generation FEPZs. This movement though significant in itself, is so far still rather hesitant.

Faced with two kinds of development, some of a basically technical nature, and others more strictly economic, the multinationals seem increasingly reluctant to move away from their markets of origin, especially since, as shown, earlier, the continual transformation of the FEPZs calls for a constant reappraisal of the choice of location. This approach would in all likelihood turn out to be too costly to be contemplated.

Obviously, one alternative is to repatriate previously redeployed activities, especially since certain manufacturing processes are undergoing changes that would favour a decision of this kind.

Thus, in the electronics field, the automation of assembly processes had tended to make it less worthwhile to establish in low-wage countries, while technological change has caused a shift in the cost structure reducing the proportion of labour costs involved in assembly[16].

In the textiles industry, increasing use is being made of highly capital-intensive production processes, in line with the automation and robotisation of manufacturing.

In future, the systematic introduction of electronic management processes will also help to free the textile industry from considerations of location governed by wage-cost levels.

In the clothing industry, the development of flexible workshops for both machining and assembly capable of adjusting to different series on short runs can only help to free a firm from wage-cost constraints.

Alongside a relaxation of wage pressures, technological and strictly commercial factors are causing market constraints to intensify.

This constraint acts first of all on goods which are sensitive to changes in social trends as in fashion : here, swift and effective contact is necessary between creative and manufacturing activities. The same applies to the manufacture of components for incorporation into highly specific manufactures, since the need to provide information so as to ensure technical conformity requires the activities concerned to be located near one another. Moreoever, to the extent that the NICs, such as Taiwan or South Korea, develop a national scientific planning system, that would promote the formation of R & D potential and the training of local engineering skills, the status of the foreign enterprise might be drastically altered. The local partner would thus be in a better position to adopt a selective attitude to imported technologies and to impose what he regards as the objective conditions for a genuine transfer of technology.

By specifying under what conditions foreign investors may use the comparative advantage afforded, governments can effectively influence the development of a specialisation in harmony with the economic structures which it wants to promote and from this stand-point, the FEPZ constitutes a preferred instrument of the industrial strategies adopted with regard to the international division of labour.

International trade would thus seem to be increasingly governed by the logic of negotiation between governments and firms. It is therefore negotiating skill and power as well as the orientation of the government's economic objectives which could lay the foundation for an advance by the countries concerned in the comparative advantage hierarchy.

NOTES

1. On the methodology see the World Bank study : Carl D. Goderez : "Planning and Implementation of Industrial Estate and Export Processing Zone Projects".

2. For example, in certain industries in Bataan local value-added tends generally to account for almost 20 per cent of the total value of exports.

3. Thus in the Masan FEPZ from 1979 to 1980 export rate fell slightly after a period of rapid growth — an apparent sign of decline.

4. See Dimitri Germidis : "Transfer of technology by multinational corporations", OECD Development Centre, Paris, 1977.

5. In : Bulletin de la Société de Banque Suisse : "La société multinationale ou l'entreprise face au monde de demain" - No. 4 - 1970.

6. On this subject see the analyses by François Perroux, in particular : "Les unités transnationales, et la rénovation de la théorie de l'équilibre général (intérieur et extérieur)", Mondes en développement No. 12, 1975.

7. P. Nugawela : "International Sub-Contracting and Free Trade Zones - Perspectives in Sri Lanka" CISIR - October 1978.

8. See the discussion of the FEPZ life cycle below.

9. D. Germidis : "International sub-contracting : a new form of investment", OECD Development Centre, 1981.

10. This does not exclude the possibility of firms established within the zone being themselves sub-contractors for principals outside the zone (parent company, another subsidiary or another independent firm). These are other forms of international sub-contracting (see D. Germidis, op. cit. and also Sivan B. "La STI : le cas des zones franches industrielles d'exportation", Doctoral thesis, University of Paris I, 1982).

11. For a discussion of the FEPZ life cycle see below.

12. See the analysis of the role of "workshop subsidiaries" in : Dimitri Germidis : "Transfer of technology by multinational corporations", op. cit.

13. Cf. O. Kreye : "World Market - Oriented industrialisation of DC's Free Production Zones and World Market Factories", op. cit.

14. See P. Judet : "Les nouveaux pays industriels", Éditions Économie et Humanisme, Collection Nord-Sud, Paris, 1981.

15. See E. Jahan, C. Jedlicki, M. Lanzzarotti and Masini, op. cit.

16. J.L. - Truel : "Les nouvelles stratégies de localisation internationale : le cas des semi-conducteurs". Revue d'économie industrielle - Fourth quarter 1980.

CONCLUSION

In the 1980s, a number of factors which helped to shape the general context of international economic activity appear to have combined to make industrial export objectives of high priority and hence prompted the proliferation of free export processing zones. Among the factors determining policies to attract export-oriented investment are the slowdown of international trade as a result of the recession in most of the economies concerned, the surge of covert or overt protectionist measures, and the now critical rate of indebtedness of many developing countries.

In fact the attraction of export-oriented foreign investment can never be an end in itself and the policies resorted to in furthrance of this aim, whatever the instruments they use — amongst them free export processing zones — are entirely governed by circumstances of time and place, and above all by the current economic phase considered in the perspective of the structures to be promoted.

As already demonstrated, it was easy to move on from import-substitution industrialisation strategies to export-based strategies. And as the case of South Korea appears to suggest, one may even turn to strategies reminiscent of the "self-reliant development" strategies which are not in fact univocal and which call on measures designed to capture both domestic and foreign markets.

This makes it all the more imperative for the FEPZ itself to evolve. Equally, it cannot be an end in itself. Since it was created with the purpose of bringing to the domestic economy the benefit of foreign contributions, its conception must obey economic exigencies that remain closely related to the changing economy of the host country and are themselves therefore subject to change. Thus, the current economic phase of the country concerned, which can be assessed only in the light of its progress toward acquiring the comparative advantage to which it reasonably aspires, will dictate its attitude to foreign investment, from which it will demand an appropriate contribution.

The lesson is clear. There is no FEPZ model which is ideal and might be generalised. In practice there are only ad hoc formulae adapted to each circumstance of time and place, which reconcile the perceived interests of the different partners.

Hence, it is impossible to expect any success from most of the FEPZ initiatives, as the majority of them have merely been copied from each other with no concern for a clear definition of the desired objectives. While, as we have seen, there are basic conditions which in general must be fulfilled regardless of the circumstances, the constraints imposed by the host country and the incentives offered must be adapted in each case in the light of the expected contribution of the investor and the requirements of national development. Otherwise, not only would FEPZs engage in a competitive battle with one another that would prove very costly in view of the limited resources of developing countries, but such competition would preclude the achievement of any objective tending to bring the present economic structure closer to the one desired. Although, as we have said, there is no generally applicable formula which would not be harmful to the host country, it is nevertheless possible to discern from the cases reviewed policy lines which can be followed to good effect in any circumstances and by any host country, in order to establish satisfactory basic conditions. We do not of course propose, to go over all the points of relevance to the main issues we are concerned with but shall merely express a few opinions that might constitute recommendations :

- So-called "open" FEPZ formulae should be encouraged, since they authorise the location which the investor considers to be the best choice — having regard to the host country's package of constraints and incentives — and allow joint use by domestic enterprises of the infrastructures provided, as well as facilitating the establishment of various relationships between the firms in the zone and those in the domestic economy besides affording greater mobility of workers.

- Joint ventures including local interests should be encouraged to set up in FEPZs ; through closer relationships between the two categories of investors subcontracting and technical cooperation agreements would be encouraged. In this way local staff might develop the enrepreneurial spirit and improve their skills.
- There should be some relaxation, at least in countries with a significant domestic market, of the restrictions on exports by FEPZ enterprises to the domestic market subject to payment of appropriate customs duties, in order to make an FEPZ location attractive.

Reconciliation of enterprise strategies with host country strategies in order to reach a "balanced arrangement" cannot be achieved without collecting sufficient information beforehand and without providing for the adjustment of the arrangement.

On the first point, the fact that the investor is often a "multinational" is not, as already stressed, devoid of significance for its strategy. Some practices involved in this strategy may have serious implications for the host country. Amongst them the multiplication of internal transactions and recourse to "transfer pricing" mechanisms are some of the more significant as they may distort the declared operating results, whether in terms of valued added, specification of external financial flows, prices of goods and services, net financial results for the year, etc.

Other "restrictive" practices may also involve matters of competition and be difficult to reconcile with the exigencies of development or quite simply the host country's perceived interests.

This being so, the importance of gathering the fullest possible information beforehand is self evident. Three types of useful, if not essential information concerning the investor can be considered :

- Information on the structure of the enterprise, its international activities, investment procedures product range, R & D and training interests, markets, etc., the fundamental strategy of the enterprise and the way in which the planned investment would tie in with that strategy, etc.
- Information on accounting methods, transfer pricing practices, overhead cost allocation methods, financing of training R & D, cost of management and technology transfer contracts, pricing of intermediates and finished products.
- Information on implantations or comparable achievements in connection with other projects, in other countries and FEPZs, the conditions under which they were carried out, the nature of relationships established with the different host countries and achieved performances, etc., any disputes that arose and the way they were settled.

Besides the foregoing information concerning the investing firm, it is also of prime importance to monitor the experience of competing host countries, particularly with regard to their FEPZs. The institutional and economic components of such countries' experience must be carefully analysed in a dynamic perspective so that the real causes of their success or failure may be recognised, the lessons to be learnt from them identified and the necessary measures taken.

Regarding the second point mentioned, concerning the need for the arrangement to be "adaptable" — at any rate if it is to be lasting and therefore "balanced" — it is increasingly obvious that in the majority of situations any investment project is carried out in an "uncertain future". Hence any "arrangement" between the investing enterprise and the host country must be capable of adjustment in the light of prevailing circumstances.

65

Two kinds of factors point to the need for adjustment :

— Factors internal to the investing enterprise such as a change in its contribution due to technical change or to changes affecting structure, organisational form or even strategy, etc. or, indeed, the experience in the host country.
— Factors external to the investing enterprise such as serious economic changes, cases of force majeure which may also arise from natural causes, changes in the legal and institutional systems of the FEPZ's host country due to a readjustement of economic policy.

It is therefore advisable for the interested parties to determine at their first contact or at the negotiation stage, the causes and conditions for adjusting their "arrangements". Obviously, the practicalities of initiating and making the adjustment may be handed over to ad hoc committees so that any negotiation would not stop the conclusion of the "arrangement", but would continue throughout its implementation. In certain situations, the parties concerned will prefer to entrust to third parties the task of adjusting their "arrangement" to changes in circumstances. Provision will be made, as the case may be, for the intervention of an arbitrator or an authorised agent.

These reflexions on the conditions for the reciprocal information of the parties concerned i.e. the host country and the investing enterprise and for reaching a "balanced arrangement" show how complex are the matters at issue and hence how difficult it is to meet the requirements of adequate and genuine information and sound negotiation.

Meeting the aforementioned requirements calls for knowledge and skills which do not lie ready to hand and which in any case call for learning and experience which cannot be improvised. The task to be accomplished is enormous, if only in terms of gathering documentation and keeping abreast of all developments. This is a task which is in fact beyond the practical possibilities of most developing countries.

Accordingly, initiatives might be taken either in the form of intergovernmental agreements or through an agency such as the World Export Processing Zones Association.

They might include setting up an international research and documentation centre with a programme comprising an inventory of successful formulae, the identification of features common to the various schemes, the study of "balanced arrangements", etc., as well as the harmonization of the technical standards to which the host country's rules and infrastructures should adhere and which in any case would serve as a reference system. They might also include the review of systems for settling disputes in the light of the types of "arrangement" considered desirable.

This centre might be backed up by an agency responsible for implementing and managing FEPZs and/or, more generally, policies for attracting export-oriented investment.

In addition, consideration might be given to the creation of an inter-governmental support and guarantee fund to cover the investing firm's risks under balanced and approved "arrangements".

Lastly, it is worthwhile pointing out that the proliferation of FEPZs in developing countries coincided with the emergence of "new forms of investment". In coming years these forms of investment may be practised with increasing frequency. This development could be due to the fact that such new forms of investment are acknowledged to be increasingly effective, particularly with regard to technology transfer — and also to the upsurge of nationalist pressures in developing countries which see appropriation of the equity of foreign firms established on their territory as more compatible with the requirements of their sovereignty and of their perceived interests. There is all the more likelihood of these developments occurring since the investing firms are encountering increased financing difficulties due to cyclical and structural reasons, while at the same time they are confronted with a worsening investment climate in the developing countries, expressed in many forms : risk of nationalisation or expropriation, of restrictions on repatriation of capital, foreign exchange restrictions, etc.

Hence, the picture one may have of an evolved form of FEPZ in future years — which may not be far distant — is that of an FEPZ resembling a "science park complex", organised and equipped by the host country and in which the investing enterprise, without investing anything apart from its know-how and technology, would have the benefit of a highly sophisticated labour force available in the FEPZ.

OECD SALES AGENTS
DÉPOSITAIRES DES PUBLICATIONS DE L'OCDE

ARGENTINA – ARGENTINE
Carlos Hirsch S.R.L., Florida 165, 4° Piso (Galería Guemes)
1333 BUENOS AIRES, Tel. 33.1787.2391 y 30.7122

AUSTRALIA – AUSTRALIE
Australia and New Zealand Book Company Pty. Ltd.,
10 Aquatic Drive, Frenchs Forest, N.S.W. 2086
P.O. Box 459, BROOKVALE, N.S.W. 2100. Tel. (02) 452.44.11

AUSTRIA – AUTRICHE
OECD Publications and Information Center
4 Simrockstrasse 5300 Bonn (Germany). Tel. (0228) 21.60.45
Local Agent/Agent local :
Gerold and Co., Graben 31, WIEN 1. Tel. 52.22.35

BELGIUM – BELGIQUE
Jean De Lannoy, Service Publications OCDE
avenue du Roi 202, B-1060 BRUXELLES. Tel. 02/538.51.69

BRAZIL – BRÉSIL
Mestre Jou S.A., Rua Guaipa 518,
Caixa Postal 24090, 05089 SAO PAULO 10. Tel. 261.1920
Rua Senador Dantas 19 s/205-6, RIO DE JANEIRO GB.
Tel. 232.07.32

CANADA
Renouf Publishing Company Limited,
Central Distribution Centre,
61 Sparks Street (Mall),
P.O.B. 1008 - Station B,
OTTAWA, Ont. K1P 5R1.
Tel. (613)238.8985-6
Toll Free: 1-800.267.4164
Librairie Renouf Limitée
980 rue Notre-Dame,
Lachine, P.Q. H8S 2B9,
Tel. (514) 634-7088.

DENMARK – DANEMARK
Munksgaard Export and Subscription Service
35, Nørre Søgade
DK 1370 KØBENHAVN K. Tel. +45.1.12.85.70

FINLAND – FINLANDE
Akateeminen Kirjakauppa
Keskuskatu 1, 00100 HELSINKI 10. Tel. 65.11.22

FRANCE
Bureau des Publications de l'OCDE,
2 rue André-Pascal, 75775 PARIS CEDEX 16. Tel. (1) 524.81.67
Principal correspondant :
13602 AIX-EN-PROVENCE : Librairie de l'Université.
Tel. 26.18.08

GERMANY – ALLEMAGNE
OECD Publications and Information Center
4 Simrockstrasse 5300 BONN Tel. (0228) 21.60.45

GREECE – GRÈCE
Librairie Kauffmann, 28 rue du Stade,
ATHÈNES 132. Tel. 322.21.60

HONG-KONG
Government Information Services,
Publications/Sales Section, Baskerville House,
2nd Floor, 22 Ice House Street

ICELAND – ISLANDE
Snaebjörn Jönsson and Co., h.f.,
Hafnarstraeti 4 and 9, P.O.B. 1131, REYKJAVIK.
Tel. 13133/14281/11936

INDIA – INDE
Oxford Book and Stationery Co. :
NEW DELHI-1, Scindia House. Tel. 45896
CALCUTTA 700016, 17 Park Street. Tel. 240832

INDONESIA – INDONÉSIE
PDIN-LIPI, P.O. Box 3065/JKT., JAKARTA, Tel. 583467

IRELAND – IRLANDE
TDC Publishers – Library Suppliers
12 North Frederick Street, DUBLIN 1 Tel. 744835-749677

ITALY – ITALIE
Libreria Commissionaria Sansoni :
Via Lamarmora 45, 50121 FIRENZE. Tel. 579751/584468
Via Bartolini 29, 20155 MILANO. Tel. 365083
Sub-depositari :
Ugo Tassi
Via A. Farnese 28, 00192 ROMA. Tel. 310590
Editrice e Libreria Herder,
Piazza Montecitorio 120, 00186 ROMA. Tel. 6794628
Costantino Ercolano, Via Generale Orsini 46, 80132 NAPOLI. Tel. 405210
Libreria Hoepli, Via Hoepli 5, 20121 MILANO. Tel. 865446
Libreria Scientifica, Dott. Lucio de Biasio "Aeiou"
Via Meravigli 16, 20123 MILANO Tel. 807679
Libreria Zanichelli
Piazza Galvani 1/A, 40124 Bologna Tel. 237389
Libreria Lattes, Via Garibaldi 3, 10122 TORINO. Tel. 519274
La diffusione delle edizioni OCSE è inoltre assicurata dalle migliori librerie nelle
città più importanti.

JAPAN – JAPON
OECD Publications and Information Center,
Landic Akasaka Bldg., 2-3-4 Akasaka,
Minato-ku, TOKYO 107 Tel. 586.2016

KOREA – CORÉE
Pan Korea Book Corporation,
P.O. Box n° 101 Kwangwhamun, SÉOUL. Tel. 72.7369

LEBANON – LIBAN
Documenta Scientifica/Redico,
Edison Building, Bliss Street, P.O. Box 5641, BEIRUT.
Tel. 354429 – 344425

MALAYSIA – MALAISIE
University of Malaya Co-operative Bookshop Ltd.
P.O. Box 1127, Jalan Pantai Baru
KUALA LUMPUR. Tel. 51425, 54058, 54361

THE NETHERLANDS – PAYS-BAS
Staatsuitgeverij, Verzendboekhandel,
Chr. Plantijnstraat 1 Postbus 20014
2500 EA S-GRAVENHAGE. Tel. nr. 070.789911
Voor bestellingen: Tel. 070.789208

NEW ZEALAND – NOUVELLE-ZÉLANDE
Publications Section,
Government Printing Office Bookshops:
AUCKLAND: Retail Bookshop: 25 Rutland Street,
Mail Orders: 85 Beach Road, Private Bag C.P.O.
HAMILTON: Retail: Ward Street,
Mail Orders, P.O. Box 857
WELLINGTON: Retail: Mulgrave Street (Head Office),
Cubacade World Trade Centre
Mail Orders: Private Bag
CHRISTCHURCH: Retail: 159 Hereford Street,
Mail Orders: Private Bag
DUNEDIN: Retail: Princes Street
Mail Order: P.O. Box 1104

NORWAY – NORVÈGE
J.G. TANUM A/S
P.O. Box 1177 Sentrum OSLO 1. Tel. (02) 80.12.60

PAKISTAN
Mirza Book Agency, 65 Shahrah Quaid-E-Azam, LAHORE 3.
Tel. 66839

PORTUGAL
Livraria Portugal, Rua do Carmo 70-74,
1117 LISBOA CODEX. Tel. 360582/3

SINGAPORE – SINGAPOUR
Information Publications Pte Ltd,
Pei-Fu Industrial Building,
24 New Industrial Road N° 02-06
SINGAPORE 1953. Tel. 2831786, 2831798

SPAIN – ESPAGNE
Mundi-Prensa Libros, S.A.
Castelló 37, Apartado 1223, MADRID-1. Tel. 275.46.55
Libreria Bosch, Ronda Universidad 11, BARCELONA 7.
Tel. 317.53.08, 317.53.58

SWEDEN – SUÈDE
AB CE Fritzes Kungl Hovbokhandel,
Box 16 356, S 103 27 STH. Regeringsgatan 12,
DS STOCKHOLM. Tel. 08/23.89.00
Subscription Agency/Abonnements:
Wennergren-Williams AB,
Box 13004, S104 25 STOCKHOLM.
Tel. 08/54.12.00

SWITZERLAND – SUISSE
OECD Publications and Information Center
4 Simrockstrasse 5300 BONN (Germany). Tel. (0228) 21.60.45
Local Agents/Agents locaux
Librairie Payot, 6 rue Grenus, 1211 GENÈVE 11. Tel. 022.31.89.50

TAIWAN – FORMOSE
Good Faith Worldwide Int'l Co., Ltd.
9th floor, No. 118, Sec. 2,
Chung Hsiao E. Road
TAIPEI. Tel. 391.7396/391.7397

THAILAND – THAILANDE
Suksit Siam Co., Ltd., 1715 Rama IV Rd.
Samyan, BANGKOK 5. Tel. 2511630

TURKEY – TURQUIE
Kültur Yayinlari Is-Türk Ltd. Sti.
Atatürk Bulvari No : 191/Kat. 21
Kavaklidere/ANKARA. Tel. 17 02 66
Dolmabahce Cad. No : 29
BESIKTAS/ISTANBUL. Tel. 60 71 88

UNITED KINGDOM – ROYAUME-UNI
H.M. Stationery Office,
P.O.B. 276, LONDON SW8 5DT.
(postal orders only)
Telephone orders: (01) 622.3316, or
49 High Holborn, LONDON WC1V 6 HB (personal callers)
Branches at: EDINBURGH, BIRMINGHAM, BRISTOL,
MANCHESTER, BELFAST.

UNITED STATES OF AMERICA – ÉTATS-UNIS
OECD Publications and Information Center, Suite 1207,
1750 Pennsylvania Ave., N.W. WASHINGTON, D.C.20006 – 4582
Tel. (202) 724.1857

VENEZUELA
Libreria del Este, Avda. F. Miranda 52, Edificio Galipan,
CARACAS 106. Tel. 32.23.01/33.26.04/31.58.38

YUGOSLAVIA – YOUGOSLAVIE
Jugoslovenska Knjiga, Knez Mihajlova 2, P.O.B. 36, BEOGRAD.
Tel. 621.992

Les commandes provenant de pays où l'OCDE n'a pas encore désigné de dépositaire peuvent être adressées à :
OCDE, Bureau des Publications, 2, rue André-Pascal, 75775 PARIS CEDEX 16.

Orders and inquiries from countries where sales agents have not yet been appointed may be sent to:
OECD, Publications Office, 2, rue André-Pascal, 75775 PARIS CEDEX 16.

68073-10-1984

OECD PUBLICATIONS, 2, rue André-Pascal, 75775 PARIS CEDEX 16 - No. 42963 1984
PRINTED IN FRANCE
(41 84 05 1) ISBN 92-64-12634-1